Assuring Quality Ambulatory Health Care: The Dr. Martin Luther King Jr. Health Center

Westview Special Studies in Health Care

Assuring Quality Ambulatory Health Care:
The Dr. Martin Luther King Jr. Health Center
edited by Donald Angehr Smith, M.D., and
Gitanjali Mukerjee, M.D.

In its ten-year existence the Dr. Martin Luther King Jr. Health Center has been pledged to quality health care and has developed detailed procedures to assure its staff and consumers that such care can and does exist. An essential part of its program has been a committee established early in the center's history to continually monitor and evaluate all aspects of the health care provided. Drs. Smith and Mukerjee describe here the various methods the committee has devised to evaluate and assure quality care. More important, they document their own experience with each method, so that other health centers and practitioners may be able to evaluate and, where necessary, improve their practices. The committee's evaluation techniques range from patient-satisfaction questionnaires to chart audits and outcome audits, and the editors include the forms they use as well as the results they produced.

Donald Angehr Smith, a graduate of the Harvard Medical School, is chief of internal medicine at the Dr. Martin Luther King Jr. Health Center and assistant professor in medicine and community health at the Albert Einstein College of Medicine.

Gitanjali Mukerjee, chief of pediatrics at the Dr. Martin Luther King Jr. Health Center and assistant professor of pediatrics at the Albert Einstein College of Medicine, received much of her education and early medical training in Bombay, India.

Also in This Series

Systems of Health Care, Douglas R. Mackintosh

Montefiore Hospital and Medical Center
Bronx, New York

Martin Cherkasky, M.D., President

The Dr. Martin Luther King Jr. Health Center

Deloris Smith, M.P.H., Project Director
Eleanor Minor, A.R.T., Director of Health Services

Assuring Quality Ambulatory Health Care: The Dr. Martin Luther King Jr. Health Center

edited by
Donald Angehr Smith, M.D., and Gitanjali Mukerjee, M.D.

Westview Press / Boulder, Colorado

Westview Special Studies in Health Care

Published in 1978 in the United States of America by
  Westview Press, Inc.
  5500 Central Avenue
  Boulder, Colorado 80301
  Frederick A. Praeger, Publisher and Editorial Director

Library of Congress Cataloging in Publication Data
Main entry under title:
Assuring quality ambulatory health care.
  (Westview special studies in health care)
    1. Clinics—Evaluation—Case studies. 2. Ambulatory medical care—Evaluation—
Case studies. 3. Ambulatory medical care—Quality control—Case studies.
4. Martin Luther King Jr. Health Center. I. Smith, Donald Angehr. II. Mukerjee,
Gitanjali. III. Series. [DNLM: 1. Evaluation studies. 2. Quality of health care.
3. Ambulatory care. WX205 A497]
RA966.S54   362.1'2   77-13225
ISBN 0-89158-409-9

Printed and bound in the United States of America

Contents

Preface ix

1. History and Overview, *Donald A. Smith, M.D.,*
   and Eleanor D. Minor, A.R.T. 1
2. Patient Questionnaire, *Liery Wynn* 13
3. Death and Drug Reaction Form, *Donald A.*
   Smith, M.D., and Gitanjali Mukerjee, M.D. 21
4. Restricted Oral Antibiotic Control Program,
   William Gordon, M.S. 29
5. Patients' Rights, *Liery Wynn*. 39
6. History of the Problem-Oriented Medical Record
   Audit, *William B. Lloyd, M.D.* 47
7. Disease Specific Audit Case History: Gonorrhea,
   Donald A. Smith, M.D. 57
8. Comprehensive Family Care Audit, *Donald A.*
   Smith, M.D., and Gitanjali Mukerjee, M.D. 65
   Instructions for Total Process 70
   Family Audit Form Instructions 71
   Family Audit Form. 77
9. Hypertension Surveillance System: An Outcome
   Approach, *Donald A. Smith, M.D., and*
   Peter L. Schnall, M.D. 83
10. Dental Care Evaluation, *Malvin F.*
    Braverman, D.M.D. 99

11. An Outside Evaluation: The Morehead Report,
      *Evaluation Unit, Department of Community
      Health, Albert Einstein College of Medicine,
      Mildred A. Morehead, M.D., M.P.H., Director* 111
12. Conclusions, *Donald A. Smith, M.D.* 143

Appendixes
      A. Problem-Oriented Medical Record Manual,
            John Allcott, M.D., and others. 151
      B. Your Rights as a Patient: A Manual (in
            English and Spanish), *Liery Wynn,
            Community Health Advocacy Department* . . .167
      C. MLK Pediatric Health Supervision Schedule
            and Forms 193
      D. Adult Health Maintenance Schedule and Forms 199
      E. Prenatal Care Protocol, *Nurse Practitioner
            Women's Health Care Committee and
            Ob-Gyn Department, Dr. Martin Luther
            King Jr. Health Department* 215
      F. Hypertension Surveillance System Materials 231

Preface

Over the past few years, the Health Care Evaluation Committee at the Dr. Martin Luther King Jr. Health Center has attempted to assure the quality of health care within the Department of Health Services. This book collects the pertinent materials we use to achieve our goals. Since 1973 we have presented some of them at meetings across the United States and have shared them with other institutions that looked to the Dr. Martin Luther King Jr. Health Center as a model. Now that these materials are available in book form, we hope dissemination will continue even more rapidly and efficiently.

I want to thank all those who have contributed their expertise as individuals or in groups from their departments. Special thanks go to Mrs. Gloria Plummer for helping to collect and arrange the materials, to Mrs. Anna Salabarria for painstakingly typing the manuscript, to Mr. Carl Fagin for his encouragement, and to Mr. Daniel Raymond Stein for his invaluable editing.

Members: Donald Angehr Smith, M.D., Chief of Internal Medicine; Mal Braverman, D.M.D., Chief of Dentistry; Mari Paul, B.S.N., Nursing Care Coordinator; Carrie Lee, Sr. F.H.W., Family Health Worker Coordinator; William Gordon, M.S., Chief Pharmacist; Antoine Moreau, M.D., Chief of Obstetrics and Gynecology; and Liery Wynn, Patients' Rights Advocate. *Ex Officio Members:* Eleanor Minor, A.R.T., Director of Health Services. *Secretary:* Mrs. Gloria Plummer

Gitanjali Mukerjee, M.D.
Chief of Pediatrics
Chairman, Health Care Evaluation Committee

1
History and Overview

Donald A. Smith, M.D.
Eleanor D. Minor, A.R.T.

The Dr. Martin Luther King Jr. Health Center (MLK) began as one of the first and largest of the Neighborhood Medical Care Demonstration Projects funded by the Office of Economic Opportunity. The site was chosen by determining where patients came from who in 1966 were using the emergency room of the Morrisania Hospital for their primary source of care. The catchment area covers health areas 24 and 26 in the South Bronx. The residents of this area are 47 percent black, 45 percent Puerto Rican, and 8 percent other. Incomes are low for those who are able to work and can find a job; the majority of the people manage on social assistance income (especially Aid to Dependent Children), social security income (the disabled or elderly), and supplemental security income.

Numerous problems existed in the health care that was available to these people prior to the establishment of MLK. Most of the available care was through hospital emergency rooms and out-patient clinics. The care tended to be episodic and symptom oriented. Long term physician-patient relationships were difficult if not impossible because of the high turnover of resident physicians in training and the fragmentation of care through numerous specialty clinics. Social services tended, practically speaking, to be inaccessible. Medical care emphasized the technical rather than the caring, nourishing aspects of medicine. At times the demeaning quality of the long trips, the long waiting, and the impersonal attention threatened to undermine the more technical medical skills which were finally brought to bear on patients' problems. At that time the local community had little or no input into the planning of care given by hospitals.

One of the purposes of MLK was to counteract some of these deficiencies in the delivery of care. A primary goal was thus to provide easily accessible, high quality, comprehensive, family-oriented long term health care to persons living in the surrounding catchment area. Another and equally important goal was to train and subsequently hire people from the community to provide personnel in the center with whom patients could easily interact. A side benefit of achieving this second goal was that federal funds would be available to the community through salaries given to health workers who lived in the neighborhood.

Early on it was thought that teams would be the most effective vehicle to accomplish the primary goal. Most physicians available at the time had specialty training in internal medicine or pediatrics and it was thought that the team would be one way in which these specialty-trained physicians could work together to deliver family care. Each team was also to have public health nurses trained in prenatal and postnatal care and well-child care. The family health worker was to be a new type of health worker hired from community residents and trained in the center in the delivery of both nursing and social services. This health worker became an important coordinator of care and was the liaison person between the patients and the physicians and nurses on the team.

In the early days of MLK, assurance of quality of care within this structure was an informal procedure. Although quality of care was a goal underlying all our developmental efforts, no systematic approach to guarantee it was provided. We relied on the professional qualifications of the providers on the teams, bolstered by occasional chart reviews performed by the medical director or by professional supervisors.

Occasionally, specific physicians' work was reviewed, prompted by the "feel" of the medical director that the practitioner was not providing care of adequate quality. Such informal audits suffered from several disadvantages. Because they were nonrandom, the work of a poor practitioner could often be missed. They were rarely performed on a large scale because of pressures of time and because of the discomfort engendered in the auditor and the audited. Considerable practitioner anxiety arose because this nonrandom informal method seemed to target certain individuals and not others. No group standards were available against which care provided by the practitioner could be judged.

A major step towards improving the quality of care was taken in 1968 with the initial implementation of the problem-oriented medical record (POMR) developed by Dr. Lawrence Weed. (Our use of POMR is described in detail in Chapter 6.) The introduction of this method was not, however, accompanied by the development of an audit process and its initial use by practitioners throughout the center was sporadic.

Formal quality of care review at MLK began in late 1971 with the establishment of the Health Care Evaluation Committee (HCEC). This committee, composed of the chiefs of medicine, pediatrics, ob-gyn, nursing, family health workers, dentistry, director of training, and the patients' rights advocate, was charged with developing a variety of types of quality of care review. Included in this book are the procedures and forms which have been utilized.

The procedures for health care evaluation are classified below into four groups, starting with the simplest to administer and ending with the most complex. The procedures for dental evaluation are described in Chapter 10.

   I.   Determination of Patient Satisfaction

   II.   Unusual Episode Review
       A. Deaths
       B. Restriction of Antibiotic Usage
       C. Patient Complaints

  III.   Process Audit through Chart Review
       A. Chart Standardization
       B. Single Disease Entity Review
       C. Comprehensive Family Chart Review

  IV.   Outcome Audit: Hypertension

Determination of Patient Satisfaction

The center developed two simple questionnaires which it periodically gave to samples of the patient population to determine how satisfied patients were with the practitioners and personnel with whom they interacted. The questionnaires and results are described in Chapter 2.

Such simple measures of patient satisfaction are important to determine the accessibility and comfort of services rendered. The drawback in such methods is that patient satisfaction is not necessarily related to the technical quality of the services. A patient may be satisfied with a practitioner who is making technically poor decisions about diagnosis and treatment. Therefore, additional systems of quality audit are needed.

Unusual Episode Review

This type of review is a systematic check of undesirable outcomes or unusual usage of certain medications. All deaths or severe drug reactions that come to the attention of any team member at MLK must be reported on a special form to the Health Care Evaluation Committee. Review of these charts will establish whether any oversight or lack of follow-up may have led to the death and whether a specific drug reaction could have been prevented. Our experience with death review and severe drug reactions is described in Chapter 3.

It was felt at the center that some antibiotics should have restricted usage because of potential toxicity, the high cost of the drug, or a limited therapeutic indication coupled with concern about increasing antibiotic resistance in certain organisms. Our experience with restricting the use of certain antibiotics is described in Chapter 4.

The development of a system to encourage and handle patient complaints has been a somewhat unique activity begun here at MLK. There is a full-time paid patient advocate whose main function is to listen to patient complaints, try to resolve the problems, and to bring them to the Health Care Evaluation Committee meeting for discussion and further action. Patients are informed of this channel of complaint by receiving a booklet at the time of registration called "Your

Rights as a Patient" (see Appendix B). Such investigations are at times rather highly charged. Most often they lead to better understanding by both patient and practitioner about the problems of communication. However, where there is gross insensitivity by a physician or other staff member, disciplinary action can and does occur. Details of this process are described in Chapter 5.

There are several problems with review of unusual incidents as a technique for maintaining quality of care. First, only the most severe errors will usually be found. Second, a physician may feel he's being "framed" by the Health Care Evaluation Committee because the selection of charts is not random. For example, a member of the Health Care Evaluation Committee may be upset with a consistently eccentric member of his subspecialty group or may disagree with his new, non-standard type of treatment for certain problems. Increased chart audit of such a practitioner may result in the discovery of more unwanted side effects of therapy solely because of the volume of charts reviewed. If these data are looked at alone, the practitioner may be unfairly condemned when compared with his colleagues.

Process Audit

The purpose of this type of audit is to look at charts as a reflection of treatment patterns both for specific diseases and for total patient care.

Chart Standardization

The first obstacle to chart review was the disorderly and illegible state of the charts. Solo practitioners may afford the luxury of a highly unique style of making notes because they alone must review their notes. However, within a group where cross coverage is important, where there may be a turnover of practitioner staff, and where several members of a team add continuing notes to the chart, legible and orderly charts are a necessity.

Although the problem-oriented medical record (POMR) was instituted at MLK in 1968, a manual detailing the process was not completed until 1974 (see Appendix A). Problem

Sheets, Flow Sheets, and Subjective-Objective-Assessment-Plan (SOAP) notes were required. To insure that such a style was implemented to the greatest measure a chart audit was performed on random afternoons by medical assistants on charts used by their practitioners. The audit process and the results are described in Chapter 6.

Single Disease Entity Review

Once a chart is auditable, one may begin to review particular disease entities. The only disease so studied by chart review at MLK to date has been gonorrhea. The process and results are documented in Chapter 7.

Single disease review as an approach to assuring quality of care is somewhat limited. Generally, the review concentrates on the technical aspects of treatment of the disease. Evaluation of the practitioner's sensitivity to what such a disease means to the patient or to his social setting is usually impossible from a single encounter on a chart. For example, each patient with gonorrhea may be treated adequately, but the fact that such a patient's contacts remain untreated or that marital dissolution is occurring may be overlooked.

Single disease review also does not permit evaluation of the type of care neighborhood health centers were set up to provide: comprehensive continuous care. Fragmentation of care, mistakes in diagnosis, failure to coordinate the total care of the patient, and the failure to be alert to psychosocial problems are examples of comprehensive health care requirements which may be missed in a single disease entity review.

Comprehensive Family Care Audit

This type of process audit is based on the periodic review of a family's chart chosen at random. The chart review is performed by one team (internist, pediatrician, nurse practitioner, family health worker) and evaluates the function of another team who is giving care to that family. This procedure is the central core of quality of care efforts at MLK. A standardized form and instructions have been designed at MLK to monitor this process (see Chapter 8).

There are several problems with such a comprehensive

family chart review. First, it requires extra effort by hard working teams to perform the review itself and then to find time to discuss the review with tightly scheduled members of the reviewed team. It also requires weekly meetings of the Health Care Evaluation Committee and seemingly endless checking of chart reviews by the chiefs of service. Most important, only a small number of charts per practitioner can be reviewed.

For example, when hypertension or obesity or diabetes is uncontrolled, should one look for a cause to the doctor, to the appointment system, to the patient, or to their mutual interaction or lack thereof? To answer this, one must look at differences in outcomes on larger numbers of patients treated by different practitioners and compare their results.

Outcome Review

To evaluate one encounter in the chart of a patient with a chronic disease and see that appropriate questions are asked and that appropriate tests and medications are ordered is only part of the issue of quality. A practitioner dedicated to avoiding any side effect of anti-hypertensive medications may have a much higher percentage of uncontrolled hypertensives than another practitioner who is more flexible in handling such side effects. The practitioner who is a nihilist about alcoholism, obesity, and smoking may have much less success in modifying these habits than one who encourages the newer behavioral approaches to such problems. The assessment of chronic disease management will not be found by looking at any single chart or patient, but only by looking at the total population of patients of one practitioner or team and comparing outcomes of treatment among themselves and with other "expert" groups of practitioners.

The Martin Luther King Jr. Health Center is now reviewing all its hypertensives in an effort to monitor on a long term basis the percentage of patients with controlled blood pressures. A detailed description of this effort may be seen in Chapter 9. It is hoped that identifying differences among practitioners will stimulate an increase in the percentage of controlled patients. Additionally, comparisons with success rates of other health care groups may encourage more effort by practitioners at MLK. Thus, for example, it was recently reported that one-third of hypertensives enrolled in the Seattle Model Cities Prepaid Health Care Project study had pressures that were uncontrolled. (*JAMA* 233:245, 1975) Is our center doing better or worse?

A review of outcome for even one chronic disease is extremely time-consuming. First, a registry of hypertensive patients must be established through review of charts of all patients registered at the center. Second, a record system must be developed to easily monitor the fraction of controlled hypertensives by team or physician on an ongoing basis. Third, the agency must have available the personnel to intensively follow-up patients whose pressures do not reflect adequate control.

The problem with such an intensive effort at controlling one chronic disease is that other important health problems may be overlooked because of lack of resources. For example, are persons on prophylactic isoniazid being followed adequately? Are all women up-to-date on Pap smears? We trust that in the future more efficient systems may be developed that will allow us to manage long term follow-up of several chronic conditions and screening procedures simultaneously. This will add a new dimension to the measurement of quality of care.

Outside Evaluation

To monitor how one is doing as an agency in quality assurance, one needs either to be able to monitor one's own success in achieving one's predetermined goals or to be able to compare oneself with similar institutions and how they perform. To initiate the former, one might tally all the health maintenance procedures done on the cumulative charts reviewed for one year to see if the agency is reaching a predetermined performance goal for each procedure. For example, are 80 percent of women up-to-date on Pap smears? Or one might have an impartial outside agency come for several days, evaluate many random charts, measure performance goals as mentioned above, and then compare these results with other health centers where they performed the same procedure.

In 1976 the Evaluation Unit of the Albert Einstein College of Medicine under the direction of Dr. Mildred Morehead evaluated MLK in comparison with over 100 other health centers. Verbatim sections of her report are reproduced in Chapter 11. Her summary of the audit of quality at MLK was as follows:

> The quality of medical care provided is excellent. As in the past, ratings in all primary care areas are above the neighborhood health center average in both assessment and maintenance care and in the management of more serious illnesses. The sole exception to this was the management of problem obstetrical patients where ratings were slightly below average.

Such outside evaluations are important because they stimulate reexamination of one's own goals of quality assurance and one's methods of monitoring them. In the area of health maintenance, for example, the Morehead report showed that the impact of tallying a number of charts over time with direct feedback to teams may be a potentially more impressive tool for change than feedback on individual charts to individual practitioners where individual deficiencies may be too often easily explained away by patient noncompliance. The fact that we do better than the average health center is less important than the jolt we received when we discovered we were not doing as well as we thought. The evaluation may have helped stimulate us to begin to go beyond individual chart review to analysis of subpopulations of charts (see, for example, Chapter 9 on hypertension).

The limits of the outside review are several. First, the agency is seen through only a few charts, e.g. 100 charts in a registered population of 40,000 people, at one point in time. Such a slice gives an important evaluation at one point in time, but may miss a trend toward improvement or deterioration in care unless it can be performed periodically, say, once every two years. More important, if part of the objective is to stimulate improvement in care within an agency, a one-time look does not assure that an agency will do anything to make the recommended changes. Too often, failure to attain certain goals may be blamed on inability to change the patient population. Above average evaluations can lull an agency into thinking it is doing well enough and it can rest on its laurels. Rather than going to an agency with a set of standards, the evaluators should request the agency's own set of quality standards prior to evaluation, such as 90 percent of children up-to-date on immunizations. The evaluation unit can then review to see if the agency is reaching its own goals, and simultaneously can evaluate the goals themselves to see if they are comparable to standards set throughout the country. In this way, the center becomes part of the evaluation and can continue to strive toward its own goals after the evaluators have left.

Cost of Financing Quality of Care Efforts

The cost of monitoring quality of care at MLK is not insignificant. The cost of the two to three hours spent by each of the eight HCEC members and the eleven hours spent by the secretary per week totaled $20,400 in 1975. In addition, the team/team audit performed eleven months out of the year by four members of each team spending approximately one hour per review cost $5,000.

These figures do not include the costs of such specific projects as gonorrhea review, the hypertensive monitoring project, the problem-oriented medical record audit, or the clinical dental evaluation. Each of these significantly raises the total cost. For example, our most expensive program has been the Hypertension Surveillance System whose main costs are for a 50 percent physician manager and the equivalent of a full-time clerk—a total of $35,000. To expand this system to include the entire center will necessitate a full-time manager costing $15,000. This person can do much of the work of the physician, but will nonetheless increase the cost of the program to $45,000. The center agreed to fund this person from patient visit income, but fortunately the state, using federal funds will provide the salary for this person under a grant from their Bureau of Disease Control. This money is not provided for quality assurance *per se*, but for a management system for better controlling hypertensives. Fortunately the ultimate objectives are the same: better controlled hypertensives.

To summarize, MLK has been spending $25,000 or 0.3 percent of its annual budget on its own quality monitoring efforts. If one adds the cost of the Hypertension Surveillance System, the annual cost rises to $60,000 or 0.7 percent of the budget. These figures are difficult to assess in terms of standard figures budgeted for quality assurance because comparable figures are unavailable. They do raise several questions:

1. What expenditure should be made by any health center on such activities; and
2. Are such efforts truly effective in maintaining high quality care?

This book does not deal with the first question, and only begins to explore the second in the chapters on gonorrhea, hypertension, and the Morehead report. Its purpose is to present our experience and our methods as baseline data from the field; as more data accumulate from other centers, these questions may be more fruitfully attacked. The forms and methods presented in this book will hopefully serve as tested models for other agencies also involved in ambulatory quality care assurance.

No formal bibliography is presented in this book. The field of ambulatory care quality assurance is young. Our activities have been generated by what we felt was necessary for our center at this time. For those interested in a bibliography of the field, a recently published review may be recommended: *Ambulatory Care Quality Assurance Project, Vol. 3, Bibliography & Selected Abstracts,* published in December 1976 by the Bureau of Quality Assurance, U.S. Dept. of HEW and available for $2.00 from the Supt. of Documents, U.S. Government Printing Office, Washington, D.C. 20402.

2
Patient Questionnaire

Liery Wynn

An early endeavor of the Health Care Evaluation Committee of the Dr. Martin Luther King Jr. Health Center was to try and assess consumer satisfaction. How did MLK patients feel about the care they were receiving? In keeping with the goals of the health center we felt that it was of the utmost importance that our patient population have a voice in the evaluation of the care they received. Patient involvement was especially important because the other evaluations that the committee was doing dealt specifically with the technical aspects of quality care. These technical forms of evaluation told us nothing about how the patients themselves felt. It's not enough to say that from a technical standpoint we gave good care to a patient or a family without also assessing the humane side of the delivery of health care. The only way that we could get an idea of the quality of human care the center was providing was to do an evaluation of patient satisfaction. Two questionnaires were developed in an effort to include patients in the health care process.

Questionnaire I (see Figure 2.1) asked the patients about their feelings toward the receptionist and each person on the team—physician, family health worker, and public health nurse. The families interviewed were those whose charts had been chosen at random for the health care evaluation. The patient grievance advocate either telephoned or visited the family to complete the questionnaire. At the meeting of the

Figure 2.1

```
                    PATIENT QUESTIONNAIRE I


        Periodically the Health Center takes a survey of patients
to find out their views about the Health Center.  The results
are distributed to the teams.  An example of one such survey
is given below.


TEAM                                               YES      NO

Do you know to what team your family belongs?      / /      / /

Do you know where your team is located?            / /      / /

Do you know the telephone extension for your
team?                                              / /      / /

RECEPTIONIST

Is the receptionist friendly?                      / /      / /

Does the receptionist address you as Ms.,
Mrs., or Mr.?                                      / /      / /

Does the receptionist make your appointment at
a convenient time?                                 / /      / /

Are you called for your appointment on time?       / /      / /

PHYSICIAN

Do you know where your doctor is located?          / /      / /

Do you always see the same doctor?                 / /      / /

Does your doctor listen to what you have
to say?                                            / /      / /

Does your doctor explain things so that
you can understand?                                / /      / /

Does your doctor speak to you in a pleasant
tone of voice?                                     / /      / /
```

Figure 2.1 (cont.)   *15*

	YES	NO
FAMILY HEALTH WORKER		
Do you know your family health worker?	/ /	/ /
Does your family health worker listen to your problems?	/ /	/ /
Does your family health worker assist you in handling your problems?	/ /	/ /
Does your family health worker assist you at home?	/ /	/ /
How often does your family health worker visit your home?	_____	
PUBLIC HEALTH NURSE		
Do you know your public health nurse?	/ /	/ /
Does your public health nurse listen to your problems?	/ /	/ /
Does your public health nurse assist you in handling your problems?	/ /	/ /
Does your public health nurse visit you at home?	/ /	/ /
How often does your public health nurse visit your home?	_____	

COMMENTS:

_____

_____

_____

_____

_____

_____

Health Care Evaluation Committee, the family's charts were evaluated and the results of the questionnaire presented.

Over a period of eighteen months, from 1969 through 1971, the questionnaire was administered to fifty-five families. There were a variety of both positive and negative responses (see Table 2.1). The majority of families felt they received good care and that team members were concerned and demonstrated a sense of understanding of their problems. The significant minority with complaints felt that their illnesses had not been explained to them in adequate detail, a receptionist had been too abrupt with them, they wished increased home visits, or they did not know who the members of their health team were.

In looking at the responses of patients contacted we had to consider the state of patient education and the fact that patients had never been involved in any way previously in the delivery of health care. This was a new concept for our patients to deal with. Many MLK patients had been provided with the basic information about their team members, including where to find them, their names, and telephone extensions but had never used the information to their advantage. The patients of the MLK had used other health facilities before. They had never been asked previously to take any role in the delivery of their health care, but submitted to whatever the health care institution felt was best for them.

TABLE 2.1
Response to Questionnaire by Heads of Households[a]

Question	Know	Don't know
Know what team they belong to	50	5
Know the name of the F.H.W.	54	1
Know the name of the P.H.N.	49	6
Know the name of the doctor	45	10
Know where their team is located	55	0
Know phone number for team office	51	4
Know the unit where doctor is located	55	0

[a]total number of family charts reviewed= 55.

The Dr. Martin Luther King Jr. Health Center believes that what patients feel and think about the care they are receiving is as important as what the professional staff feels it should be. We might think that we did a good job, but the patient could have a very different view of the care we provided.

Questionnaire II was an evaluation of physicians (see Figure 2.2). Fifteen families were picked at random to participate in this evaluation. Each was mailed the physician questionnaire and asked to fill it out and return it to the center. Of the fifteen questionnaires sent out, ten were returned completed, three were returned because of wrong addresses, and two were never answered.

The results indicated that three quarters of the patients perceived the doctor as having a satisfactory understanding of them and their problems. The remainder either did not know who their physician was or had some negative feeling toward him. This questionnaire has not been administered again and there is no current plan to reinstitute it. In a health center that provides team care, it seems somewhat inappropriate to focus so much attention on just one member of the team.

The Health Care Evaluation Committee believes that patient evaluation of team care is important. The procedure of questioning families about their feelings towards the health care provided by their team at the center, Questionnaire I, was discontinued when chart audit was changed to the more complex team-team review. Writing this book has stimulated the Health Care Evaluation Committee to design a new patient questionnaire for future implementation. The new questionnaire will cover a wider range of questions. It will not be confined to knowledge of team members, where they are located, and how they may be reached. We now know more about what we need to know as well as about what's important to our patient population and thus we can develop a more detailed questionnaire.

The new questionnaire will give us a more detailed look at each team member as well as at the overall services that the health center provides. It will also inquire about administrative

Figure 2.2

```
                        QUESTIONNAIRE II


                                                    YES        NO
        Do you know who your doctor is?             / /        / /

        Do you always see the same doctor for
        appointments on the units?                  / /        / /

        Does your doctor listen to what you have
        to say?                                     / /        / /

        Does your doctor explain about your health
        or illness in a way that you can understand? / /       / /

        Does your doctor explain all medications and
        laboratory slips to you?                    / /        / /

        Does your doctor speak to you in a pleasant
        voice and a respectful manner?              / /        / /

        Are you satisfied with the care he or she is
        giving you?                                 / /        / /

        Do you think his or her professional manner
        can be improved? (If yes, please explain how) / /      / /

        Do you and your family take the medicines
        that your doctor prescribes for you? (If not,
        why?)                                       / /        / /

        Do you feel that your doctor is really
        concerned about you and your health?        / /        / /

        Do you feel that your doctor is only doing
        his/her job because they are being paid to
        do so?                                      / /        / /

        At the end of your appointment does he/she
        usually ask you if you have any questions
        or if there is anything that you don't
        understand?                                 / /        / /

        Your doctor's name (only if you wish to include it)_____

        Other comments you may wish to make:_____

        _____

        _____

        _____
```

changes like the new billing system. (During the period that we used the first questionnaire there was no charge for services. Now that we have begun to charge a fee for service we need some method to evaluate the billing department.)

Another area of concern will be comparison of services. Basically, we want to have an idea of how our patients' perceptions of MLK services compare with those of other hospitals, clinics, and private doctors that our patients have used in the past as well as any other health care facility they may be using concurrently with MLK. Finally, we want to know how our patients feel about the services offered and the things that they would like to see changed.

Assessing consumer satisfaction, which we have done and intend to do more extensively, is a useful form of evaluating health care. Even though consumers may be "satisfied" where the professional perceives gaps (most obvious in some of the elderly, who were delighted with their care despite clear omissions in actual medical care revealed by the charts), the answers to the many questions submitted by the problem of how patients perceive and feel about the care they receive are important. Although technical quality care is important, the ultimate goal of our endeavors is human well-being. Each patient seen has some insight about this that can be invaluable to persons providing care.

3

Death and Drug Reaction Form

Donald A. Smith, M.D.
Gitanjali Mukerjee, M.D.

The detailed examination of patients dying under one's care is a time honored tradition within the medical profession. Such examinations have been used as tools to broaden the physician's outlook about possible preterminal diagnosis and to judge whether preterminal intervention was useless, harmful, or helpful. Although death conferences and clinico-pathologic conferences have been used primarily within the in-patient setting, we decided to see if death reviews would also be useful educational tools within the out-patient setting. Similarly, we decided to ask for reports about adverse side effects of medications as a means to educate practitioners about the possible harmful side effects of therapeutic intervention.

In 1968, the Health Care Evaluation Committee at the Dr. Martin Luther King Jr. Health Center devised a Death and Drug Reaction Form (see Figure 3.1). The form was to be completed by any team member who learned about the death of a patient cared for by his team. Physicians were asked to report adverse drug reactions on the same form. After the HCEC reviews a death report, the appropriate chief of service reviews the chart in light of the conditions of death to see if antemortem health care was appropriate. Any problems in care are referred back to the individual practitioner responsible by the chief of the appropriate service or the chairman of the HCEC. Hospital deaths may need to

Figure 3.1

TEAM
ID #
NAME
ADDRESS
D.O.B.

TELEPHONE NO.

Age_____

REPORT OF DEATH ☐ OR MAJOR DRUG REACTION ☐ FORM

Date of death or drug reaction _____
Date of notification to team _____
By whom: _____
Date received by HCEC _____
Date completed by HCEC _____

Internist_____ Pediatrician:_____

P.H.N.:_____ F.H.W.:_____

CIRCUMSTANCES CONCERNING DEATH OR MAJOR DRUG REACTION:

COMMENTS (include cause, place, ME report, etc.)_____

COMMENTS BY H.C.E.C._____

be reviewed with the appropriate chairman of the hospital department on whose services the death occurred. After a chart has been reviewed it is sent for microfilming and removed from the active clinic files.

Several problems in the death review process have become apparent. At first it seemed that many deaths were not being reported. Charts of people who had died two to three years earlier would occasionally be found by team members as they reviewed their case loads. To broaden the sources of information about deaths, a list of persons living in the MLK catchment area who had autopsies performed by the city medical examiner is sent to MLK by the New York City Department of Health. Charts of people on this list who have received care at MLK are then pulled and examined by the HCEC. This source of information has increased somewhat the number of deceased patients who have been reviewed.

Another initial problem was that the cause of death reported on the form was often "unknown." This was partly because the responsibility for reporting deaths lay mainly with family health workers rather than physicians. The HCEC began returning many of the death reports to the teams for more information. Physicians were requested to hold the reports until they received the results of autopsies performed on the deceased, reviewed hospital notes, or discussed the details of death with family observers. Recently, MLK has established a procedure for obtaining autopsies directly from the medical examiner rather than relying on each physician to obtain them himself. The quality of the death reports has begun to improve.

From early 1974 through January 1976 the HCEC reviewed 138 death reports. The years of patients' deaths are listed in Table 3.1, and Table 3.2 gives the age and sex for the reported deaths. The causes of the 138 deaths, in order of decreasing frequency, were as follows:

Unknown causes	34
Known causes	104
Total	138

Cardiac	26	Myocardial infarction: 14, Congestive heart failure (including rheumatic valvular disease, hypertension, cardiomyopathy): 11, Unspecified: 1
Cancer	25	Lung: 4, Colon: 4, Uterine: 3, Larynx: 1, Brain: 1, Esophagus: 1, Leukemia: 1, Vulvar: 1, Prostate: 1, Unspecified: 8
Pulmonary	13	Pneumonia: 4, Tuberculosis: 1, Asthma: 2, Chronic obstructive pulmonary disease: 2, Pulmonary infarction from embolization: 3, Chronic interstitial fibrosis: 1
Alcohol-related	10	Liver failure: 5, Pancreatitis: 2, "Acute Intoxication:" 1, "Chronic alcoholics found dead:" 2
Homicide	9	
Stroke	6	
Accidental	6	Two children fell out of windows, one child asphyxiated on a balloon, one adult died in an auto accident, one teenager drowned, and one elderly man died in a motorcycle accident
Suicide	3	
Renal failure	2	
Miscellaneous	4	Infection of the central nervous system—type unspecified: 1, Childbirth: 1, Fractured hip: 1, "Diabetic coma:" 1

TABLE 3.1

Year of death	Number of death reports reviewed
1972	3
1973	8
1974	29
1975	70
1976 (January only)	3
No date given on report	25
Total	138

TABLE 3.2

Age (years)	Number of deaths Males	Females
0-1	0	1
2-9	2	2
10-19	3	3
20-29	4	4
30-39	2	3
40-49	9	12
50-59	11	13
60-69	5	13
70-79	13	19
80- +	6	10
Unknown	2	1
Subtotals	57	81
Overall total	138	

Adverse drug reactions have only been reported twice in the last two years. One involved a switch in similar sounding drugs. Aldactone, a diuretic with a mild anti-hypertensive effect was prescribed, but the patient was given Aldomet, a much more potent anti-hypertensive. The patient soon became weak and dizzy and notified the practitioner, who found the mistake and notified the HCEC immediately. The chief pharmacist reviewed the situation and found the bottles of Aldactone and Aldomet stored side by side. He separated the two medications on the shelves and cautioned the pharmacy staff to avoid similar problems in the future.

It is difficult to draw firm conclusions from the above presentation of the demographic data about deaths at MLK. Because it is impossible to determine the size of the population at risk, the year of death in some cases, the cause of death in others (25 percent of cases), and whether these 138 cases represent all deaths of patients registered at MLK, comparative analysis of our figures with national figures is impossible. Such a continued look at deaths does, however, make us painfully aware that 24 percent of the deaths in which a cause is known occur in categories in which traditional delivery of medical services has little effect: alcohol-related, homicide, and accidental. Unlike the review of deaths in hospital settings, which focuses on the rare and unusual diseases, out-patient death review focuses attention on the all too common forms of mortality for which currently available better diagnostic and even therapeutic skills seem irrelevant.

More important than the overall view of deaths at MLK has been an analysis on an individual basis of the relation of care received to the cause and course of death. Several cases of uncontrolled hypertensives dying from acute left ventricular failure have been used to demonstrate to teams the crucial importance of rapid and sustained control of blood pressure. Another case involved a Ms. V., age 18, who committed suicide. She was referred to psychiatric care on three occasions but had not kept any of the appointments. From the chart review, it was apparent that the team and primary physician were unaware of the delinquent appointments and the absence of follow-up care for this depressed patient. A mechanism was then instituted with the mental health coordinator to inform the practitioners about mentally ill patients who have missed psychiatric appointments.

One gentleman died of rectal carcinoma. Review of his chart revealed that stool testing for occult blood had not been ordered as required by our health maintenance protocol. It was pointed out to the practitioner involved and all internists that if this health maintenance procedure had been performed, this man's rectal carcinoma might have been found at an earlier stage. Review of the charts of many patients dying of cancer has shown confusion about the responsibility of the primary care physician and that of the oncologist or radiotherapist at the hospital guiding the therapy. Some patients choose to solely use the oncologist, as an absence of notes from the MLK practitioner in the chart for six months prior to death reveals. Other patients go to both physicians, with consequent confusion about who is doing what. Better collaboration between the internist group at MLK and the Oncology Department at Montefiore Hospital should resolve this problem.

Review of one elderly woman's death revealed that she had died suddenly in home after climbing seventeen flights of stairs because the project elevators were out of order. The team internist had already written four letters unsuccessfully requesting the housing authority to move the woman to a lower floor because of her frequent angina. This incident stimulated direct communication asking the borough president to investigate and to allow some provision for movement of people within public housing who have significant health problems.

Although the above examples make one deeply upset over problems within our health system, having a committee which can consistently review such charts and make significant changes in the system to prevent recurrences is a major asset and necessity for any health center. Few other events within a doctor-patient relationship have a greater emotional impact or have more potential for making changes in a physician's and agency's behavior than a patient's death. Poor care, of course, is the exception. One of the prime functions for the HCEC should also be to give due praise to those practitioners and teams who often extend themselves dramatically to help individuals and families face the stark reality of imminent death.

4
Restricted Oral Antibiotic Control Program

William Gordon, M.S.

Anti-microbial drugs are the most commonly prescribed medications in the United States. They are dispensed about twice as often as tranquilizers, the next most commonly used class of prescription drugs. The dramatic successes of appropriately used antibiotics in treating acute bacterial infections account for the great popularity of these agents among both physicians and patients. With the exception of psychiatrists, almost all doctors involved in direct patient care prescribe anti-microbial agents. Unfortunately, patient pressure for antibiotic treatment of viral or minor infections and aggressive sales efforts by pharmaceutical companies have resulted in significant abuse of these valuable agents.

In addition to cost and toxicity risk to the individual patient, the excessive use of antibiotics is a potent selective force favoring general emergence of resistant bacteria, thereby threatening the future effectiveness of our antibiotic armamentarium. It is often hard for the physician to think in these terms when faced with a demanding patient or a situation which might be caused by an infectious agent. However, it is clear that the emergence of resistant bacteria during the last fifteen years was in large part caused by our failure to develop a stronger public health awareness about the consequences of antibiotic abuse. The Oral Antibiotic Drug Release Form and the recommendations for its use were designed to discourage the inappropriate use of antibiotics and to promote the appropriate use of these often valuable agents.

Developing an Oral Antibiotic Drug Release Form

The Dr. Martin Luther King Jr. Health Center Formulary lists the following oral antibiotic agents, which are the antimicrobial drugs of choice for most common infectious states and can be prescribed at the discretion of the practitioner: (1) Penicillin-G, (2) Penicillin-V, (3) Ampicillin, (4) Dicloxacillin, (5) Erythromycin, (6) Tetracycline, (7) Sulfisoxazole, (8) Methenamine, and (9) Nitrofurantoin. In January 1975, three comparatively new and expensive antibiotic agents were proposed for inclusion in the MLK Drug Formulary: Cephalexin (Keflex); Clindamycin (Cleocin); and Trimethaprim/Sulfamethoxazole (Septra). These new agents were discussed at a series of formulary meetings. It was decided that they would be approved for addition to the formulary as restricted antibiotics. The reasons for restricting and monitoring use of each of these antibiotics were as follows.

1. Cephalexin (Keflex): Cephalosporins have been used as alternatives to penicillins in patients allergic to penicillins, but they can also induce hypersensitivity reactions, and there is some cross-sensitivity with penicillins.
2. Clindamycin (Cleocin): Clindamycin can cause severe colitis which may end fatally. Therefore, it should be reserved for serious infections where less toxic antimicrobial agents are inappropriate.
3. Trimethaprim/Sulfamethoxazole (Septra or Bactrim): May cause hemolysis in glucose-6-phosphate dehydrogenase deficient individuals.

MLK does not have a Division of Infectious Disease. Thus, some mechanism for monitoring and evaluating the new agents was needed. To initiate this, a Restricted Oral Antibiotic Control Program was developed by the pharmacy, working in conjunction with the Health Care Evaluation Committee. To implement the program properly, a form had to be designed which when completed could supply the information necessary for the Restricted Oral Antibiotic Control Program. Many forms were drafted but most were too complicated. The form eventually chosen was approved for use by both the Pediatric and the Internal Medicine Committees. The form with instructions for use are on pages 32 and 33.

The form lists the antibiotics and the indications for which they may be prescribed. A practitioner writing a prescription for these antibiotics must complete the form and have the patient present it along with the prescription to the pharmacy. The completed form authorizes the pharmacist to dispense the restricted antibiotic. A copy of the form is sent by the pharmacy to the Formulary Committee. An evaluation of restricted antibiotic usage is then conducted by the committee with the focus on maximizing "rational drug therapy." In certain cases, discussions between prescribing physicians and members of the committee may then take place to further clarify the drug usage. In all instances when a physician indicates on the form the need for a restricted antibiotic for other than the designated indications, the pharmacist verifies with the prescribing physician the need for the drug prior to dispensing. If the physician reiterates the need for the antibiotic for those indications, it is dispensed by the pharmacist and so noted on the form. These situations are then reviewed by the Formulary Committee.

Results

The results of the Restricted Oral Antibiotic Control Program have been tabulated in terms of the number of prescriptions dispensed, the number of units dispensed per each drug, and the number of units per each indication. No comparative study could be made because the drugs were not available at MLK prior to the initiation of the Oral Antibiotic Drug Release Form. The figures below are based on a utilization study for the period from January 1975 through December 1975.

Cephalexin (Keflex) Capsules

Eighty-one prescriptions were dispensed for Keflex capsules, sixty-seven of which were for urinary tract infections and thirteen were for either otitis media or pneumonia. One prescription written for a staphylococcal skin infection was changed by the physician from Keflex capsules to Dicloxacillin capsules because of the questionable indication. The pharmacist checked with the physician to ascertain whether he had tried the "drug of first choice." In this case, a penicillinase-resistant penicillin such as Dicloxacillin should have been tried first. Occasional strains of coagulase-positive staphylococci may be resistant to cephalosporins. The physician concurred and authorized changing the prescription to dicloxacillin.

The Restricted Oral Antibiotic Drug Release Form
Instructions for Completing the Form

Physician:
1. Checks antibiotic to be prescribed and indication for its use.
2. Prints his name, date, unit, and phone extension.
3. Writes prescription and gives patient both the form and the prescription to bring to the pharmacy.
4. If the physician feels that the drug is to be used for an indication other than those stated on the form, it must be specified in writing on the form in the space designated.

Unit Staff:
1. Form should be addressograph plated as the prescription is. If plate not available, print patient information in the provided box. Instruct patient to bring both form and prescription to the pharmacy.

Pharmacist:
1. The completed form and prescription will authorize the pharmacist to dispense the restricted antibiotic prescribed.
2. When the form is completed by the physician checking the "drug" and "indication" boxes, the pharmacist writes "drug dispensed" in the space labeled "action taken" and prints his name and the date.
3. When the form is completed by the physician checking only the drug and writing a different indication, the pharmacist shall confirm the stated indications with the physician (phone) whereby the drug may be changed to a non-restricted antibiotic. In either case, the "action taken" space must be completed.
4. When the prescription is processed, print the prescription number on the form and file it in the pharmacy office for forwarding to the Formulary Committee.

Figure 4.1

DR. MARTIN LUTHER KING JR. HEALTH CENTER
3674 Third Avenue — Bronx, New York 10456

DEPARTMENT OF HEALTH SERVICES   DIVISION OF PHARMACY SERVICES

RESTRICTED ORAL ANTIBIOTIC DRUG RELEASE

The following drugs are restricted for use and may be dispensed by the Pharmacy on prescription only if accompanied by this completed form. The physician must check the drug required and must check indications for use or note other specific indications.

(PLATE)

▱ CEPHALEXIN (Keflex)
INDICATIONS:

▱ Urinary tract infection due to organism shown to be resistant by sensitivity testing to other agents including Ampicillin, Sulfonamides, Tetracycline, or where use of these other drugs is contraindicated.**
▱ OTHERS

▱ CLINDAMYCIN (Cleocin)
INDICATIONS:
▱ Moderate to severe Staphylococcal soft tissue infection which requires antibiotic therapy in patients allergic to Penicillin.
▱ OTHERS

▱ TRIMETHAPRIM/SULFAMETHOXAZOLE(Septra, Bactrim)
INDICATIONS:
▱ 1. Urinary tract infection due to organism shown to be resistant by sensitivity testing to other agents, including - Ampicillin, Cephalosporins, Sulfonamides and Tetracycline or where use of these other drugs is contraindicated.**
▱ 2. Prolonged suppressive therapy for chronic recurrent urinary tract infection (as a secondary alternative to Methenamine Mandelate or Hippurate).
▱ 3. Chronic prostatitis. ▱ OTHER:

**Contraindications may include (1) Allergy to any of the Antibiotics. (2) For Sulfonamides G-6PD deficiency, and pregnancy at term. (3) For Tetracycline - last half of pregnancy, age under 10 years, renal failure or liver disease.

PRINT PHYSICIAN NAME_____DATE_____UNIT_____EXT._____

Action Taken: PHARMACY_____
_____
_____

PRINT PHARMACIST NAME_____DATE_____

RESTRICTED ORAL ANTIBIOTIC DRUG RELEASE FORM

Approximately twenty-two prescriptions for Keflex capsules were issued by various physicians without the necessary form being completed. Upon being advised that the pharmacy could not dispense the medication without the completed form, twelve of these prescriptions were changed to a non-restricted antibiotic.

Of the total eighty-one prescriptions dispensed, sixty-five were initiated at MLK and sixteen were issued as continuations of cephalosporin treatments started during hospitalization, usually post-operative. The totals dispensed were 3,040 capsules 250 mg. for UTI's; 414 capsules 250 mg. other ($30/100); 364 capsules 500 mg. ($60/100).

Clindamycin (Cleocin)

Seven prescriptions were written for Cleocin capsules (150 mg.). Three of these were for moderate to severe staphylococcal soft tissue infection requiring therapy in patients allergic to penicillin. The other four prescriptions were written for resistant acne infections. All were written by the same physician. The average number of capsules dispensed per acne prescription was 100 capsules at a cost of 25 cents per capsule. When the physician was challenged on the use of Cleocin for acne, he was able to document that the drug was useful for tetracycline-resistant acne and that major toxic effects at this dosage were rare. Based on this, he prepared an Acne Treatment Protocol which was discussed and approved by all the internists at one of their weekly meetings.

The total number of Cleocin capsules dispensed for the seven prescriptions was 554.

Trimethaprim/Sulfamethoxazole (Septra or Bactrim)

Forty prescriptions were written and dispensed for Septra tablets, sixteen of which were for Urinary Tract Infections due to organisms shown to be resistant by sensitivity testing to other agents such as Ampicillin, Cephalexin, Sulfisoxazole, and Tetracycline or where their use was contraindicated. Thirteen prescriptions were for prolonged suppressive therapy for chronic recurrent urinary tract infections as a secondary alternative to Methenamine. Five Septra prescriptions were written for chronic prostatitis and six prescriptions were continuations of therapy which originated elsewhere.

The total number of Septra tablets dispensed during the study period was 2,000 at a cost of $19/100 tablets.

Resistances

The emergency room at MLK has been the primary source of resistance to the program. During those hours when the primary-care units are closed, the emergency room becomes the sole source of patient care. The emergency room is staffed by "moonlighters" (practitioners who work on a part-time *per diem* or contingent basis, on week-ends, holidays, and nights and who otherwise have no involvement in agency affairs). These "moonlighters" bring with them their unique and sometimes idiosyncratic habits of practice and prescribing. They usually have not bothered to familiarize themselves with MLK's protocols and treatment standards, or with the drug formulary and related prescribing procedures. The moonlighters usually prescribe according to the methods of their previous place of employment, which may have been a "Medicaid Mill" in an urban ghetto, a proprietary hospital in the midwest, a private group practice in the suburbs, or a clinic in Calcutta. The pharmacist who is on duty when the moonlighters are in session is in a constant state of consternation, faced with a prescription flow that does not conform to MLK policy.

Antibiotics make up a major portion of the medications prescribed in the emergency room. A moonlighting practitioner may prescribe an antibiotic on a particularly busy night without the aid of laboratory test results and without consulting the patient's chart. If in his previous place of employment the prescribing philosophy was one of "overkill," the immediate utilization of the strongest and most potent drug of any given classification, then a Cephalosporin might be used for an otherwise uncomplicated urinary tract infection which probably would have responded just as well to Ampicillin at a fraction of the cost. If the practitioner was accustomed to a research-oriented teaching hospital environment, he might want to prescribe a new or investigational drug with little or no record of clinical experience.

Prior to the use of the Restricted Oral Antibiotic Release Form, the pharmacist would receive an antibiotic prescription and would either fill it and assume that the practitioner had done the proper work-up, or refuse to fill it and prepare himself for a bitter confrontation. With the advent of the program the onus has shifted to the practitioner and confrontations are apt to be humorous rather than bitter.

One incident in particular, which was celebrated by the entire pharmacy staff as a moral victory, had as its foil a rather sophisticated moonlighter who seemed to ooze an air of "prominent private practice." He insisted that the prescription he had written for Clindamycin be dispensed without the Release Form being filled in, strictly on the basis of his self-perceived importance. The pharmacist stood his ground and would not dispense the drug without the necessary form being completed. The practitioner finally acquiesced and filled in the pertinent information, which included various drug allergies and detailed organism sensitivities. All the criteria met, the pharmacist had no choice but to go ahead and prepare the prescription, even though he suspected that the doctor had contrived a fictitious case history. During the course of their conversation the doctor asked the pharmacist what the purpose of the form was. When the pharmacist casually mentioned that it would be reviewed by the Formulary Committee, the doctor suddenly remembered that "Erythromycin might just do the trick." He then took back the completed form, ripped it in half, and without a single word, returned to the emergency room.

Conclusion

The restricted Oral Antibiotic Control Program has proved a viable and facile means of attaining rational and justifiable utilization of newer anti-microbial agents. Although no comparative study could be made of cost reductions, the existence of the form and its particulars has deterred some practitioners from inappropriately prescribing the antibiotics in question. Probably the most beneficial development derived from the program so far is the demonstration that the adverse trends described in the opening paragraph can be altered. Through the combined efforts and resources of the pharmacy and the internists, a significant evaluatory tool was developed at MLK and has enhanced its system of health-care delivery.

5
Patients' Rights

Liery Wynn

The Dr. Martin Luther King Jr. Health Center as it existed in the years from 1967 to 1969 stemmed from a dream that Dr. Harold Wise had while he served as a resident at Morrisania City Hospital and was in charge of home care there. A Canadian, Dr. Wise had strong sympathies for the disadvantaged. It grieved him to see poor people waiting in city hospital emergency rooms, sometimes in droves after traveling long distances, for care by overworked and underpaid resident staffs. To give at least some fraction of the disadvantaged access to a first class health center staffed by caring personnel was Dr. Wise's objective.

Unfortunately, even at MLK, not all personnel shared Dr. Wise's vision or were as charitable in their thinking. Abrasive staff attitudes and behaviors sometimes caused problems for patients. In the summer of 1969, in line with its democratic ideals of upgrading and humanizing health care and to further realize Dr. Wise's dream, MLK set up an innovative patient advocacy program. This program represented a considerable departure from the traditional attitudes in health care institutions, most of which did not even recognize the existence of patients' rights *per se*.

One result of the program was a patients' rights pamphlet. In July 1969, the first draft of this pamphlet, "Your Rights as a Patient," was put together. (See Appendix B for the final version.) The main concern in the draft was to express the moral right of a patient to be treated as a human being. Patients already knew about such legal rights as malpractice and informed consent for treatment. The problem was how to allow patients to air and solve their human complaints. For example, how do you encourage a patient to complain if a receptionist yells at him?

I decided to solicit from the patients and the staff of the health center their ideas about rights they felt patients should have. I also wanted to explore how the staff felt about patients having rights *per se*. The next six months were spent talking to patients in the streets, waiting rooms, PTA's and community groups, and interviewing health center staff. The resulting pamphlet focuses on the right to privacy, dignity, confidentiality, and appointments.

The patients' rights covered in MLK's pamphlet include many often ignored in other clinics. Among these are the right to courtesy and respect, the right to refuse treatment, the right to clear explanations (including the right to clear explanations about possible side effects of medicines), the right to request a different physician, the right to privacy (for example, one should not be questioned about Medicaid in public), the right to choose the time for an appointment, the right to transportation to and from the center when disabled, and the right to assistance in applying for Medicaid.

The patients' rights pamphlet makes it clear that many decisions at the center are not necessarily technical or medical. For example, the process of deciding when the center should be open is entirely different from deciding when to remove an appendix. Confidentiality is not a technical issue, but rather an issue of individual rights.

Along with patients' rights come patients' responsibilities. Patients are asked to be responsible for those things that help the health center provide better care for them. These include keeping appointments, telling center personnel about treatment received from other doctors or clinics, and informing staff if a prescribed course of medication cannot be followed.

In March 1970 we began to distribute the pamphlet to patients, community residents, community agency staff, health center staff, and other interested people. Our goals were to enable health center patients to learn their rights as patients and what they could do to secure those rights, and to improve the relationship between patients and staff at the health center.

From March 1970 to May 1970 only the staff at MLK were involved in the orientation. We wanted first to try and iron out any problems among the staff. We met separately with each group of employees: the dentists, physicians, medical assistants, family health workers, public health nurse, and each subsequent group of trainees. Some staff felt that patients should not be told that they had rights. Others felt threatened because patients would be questioning them about the care they would be giving. Our position was that these specific rights were included in the basic right that patients already have: to be treated as human beings. Furthermore, if staff were giving proper care, there would be no problems.

The orientation demonstrated that stronger influences would have to be applied to insure these rights for our patients. I went to the administration and explained the feelings of some of the employees. A decision was reached to send a memo to all staff from the office of the project director emphasizing that all the rights in the pamphlet were now official health center policy.

In July 1970, orientation began for the patients. The Community Health Advocacy Department found that people seldom read material received in the mail. We decided to try and reach in person as many people as we could. We held apartment meetings by setting up tables in the housing projects on the first and sixteenth of the month. We also had the family health workers distribute the pamphlet while on home visits and in the lobby of the health center.

The personal approach to distribution allowed us to give the patients a brief explanation of the rationale for the pamphlet. We were also interested in their reactions to the new procedure. Using the above methods, we reached about 5,000 of the 7,000 families registered in the MLK area.

Complaint Procedure

To insure that patients have a mechanism to voice their complaints I was selected as patient advocate. My first step

was to develop a complaint procedure. The complaint procedure is designed to resolve problems in the quickest way
possible. First, the patient is urged to speak with any employee he feels has abridged his rights as soon as it happens.
If this proves unsatisfactory, the patient can fill out a complaint form or call the patient advocate, who is responsible
for handling such a situation.

When contacted, the patient advocate uses a four stage
procedure to resolve the complaint.

Stage One	The patient advocate receives or fills out a complaint form. This includes a narrative of the complaint and the name or names of the staff involved. The patient advocate then meets with the staff involved in the incident.
Stage Two	If this meeting does not resolve the issue, the patient advocate takes the complaint to the staff member's supervisor. The supervisor must report a decision and action to the patient advocate within five days. The patient advocate then relays the information to the patient.
Stage Three	If the patient is still dissatisfied, the patient advocate schedules a conference among himself, the patient, the staff involved, and either the department head or supervisor.
Stage Four	If issues are not resolved at this stage, and several patients have made similar complaints about the staff or situation, the patient advocate recommends change to the project director.

Although patients were initially fearful, complaints
nevertheless began to come in. The most common fear of
patients was that if they complained about a doctor he would
give them the wrong medication the next time they saw him.
From 1971 through 1976, I received about 1,200 complaints,
an average of 240 a year. The kinds of patient complaints
ranged from grievances against specific employees to those

against administrative policies. A rough percentage distribution follows.

Kinds of Complaints	Percentage
Specific employee	60
Dignity	20
Health center policy	10
Confidentiality	2
Other	8
Total	100

An instance of the commonest kind of complaint, that against a specific employee, occurred when a female patient with a vaginal discharge was seen by a physician who told her that she had a positive smear for gonorrhea and treated her with penicillin. The patient went home and told her husband, who then had a gonorrheal culture taken which came back negative. The patient subsequently found out that her smear was probably a false positive, because her culture turned out negative. Meanwhile, the anxieties aroused by this situation led to the couple's separation. Luckily I was able to meet with the two of them, get the problem straightened out, and thus end this temporary separation.

The seemingly simple problem became complicated because neither of these patients knew anything, nor were they informed, about how gonorrheal tests are done. Consequently, they did not know that the smear was not the most conclusive test for gonorrhea, nor that smears often are falsely positive. After explaining this to both patients, the problem was resolved.

This was typical of the cases that had to be dealt with after some damage had been done to a family situation. These problems could often have been avoided if only someone had taken the time to explain all the possibilities of this test. Of all the various complaints registered, I think that poor education of patients with positive gonorrheal smears has had the most negative impact on the delivery of health care which is supportive of family structure. The same kind of complaint still comes up occasionally, but not as often as formerly.

Patient dignity was the issue in numerous complaints about a physician in the eye clinic. This physician was accused of having a very "negative attitude," displayed in a number of ways, from how he talked to patients to his constant tardiness for sessions. He also left before seeing all of his scheduled patients. Following the complaint procedure of the health center, I spoke to the physician on several occasions, along with his supervisor. The physician did not change his attitude or behavior, and the complaints against him continued. Finally, he was fired by the health center.

One of the most important rights protected at MLK is confidentiality of patient information. Confidentiality encourages full disclosure of information by a patient to the medical professional or other member of the health team. If patients know that what they tell a doctor, family health worker, or nurse will go no further than the members of the team without their consent, they will be encouraged to provide the information necessary for proper diagnosis and treatment. On the other hand, if the patients hear that highly personal information about their medical problems is being circulated among employees or visitors without their knowledge or notification, they will be reluctant to make future disclosures, and will be justifiably indignant. There is no reason, for example, why even "highly placed" visitors should be allowed to sit in on conferences without the patient's permission.

To protect confidentiality the following guidelines were established. Visitors invited to patient care conferences without patient consent are limited to those called in by the team for necessary medical consultation. All other visitors and agencies must have informed patient consent. The patient has the right to see letters and to know about conferences and the results of conferences. Also, the patient must sign all letters. An example of an employee violating the confidentiality of a patient occurred when a patient stated that an employee had given a neighbor information from her record. After investigating the complaint, I found it was true. The employee was given a warning notice.

Some patients complained that preference was shown in treating the families of certain employees at the health center. For example, some female employees would show up in gynecology clinic and be seen immediately, bypassing patients waiting with appointments. This problem was remedied by not permitting employees to be seen during working hours except in emergencies.

Less common complaints included lack of respect shown by employees toward patients, giving prescriptions without explaining their possible side effects, and lack of coordination between physicians and the pharmacy, causing confusion about the size of prescriptions ordered and the number of refills allowed. The prescription problems were brought to the attention of the medical director and the pharmacy director. The solution was to pre-pack medication in accordance with the amount needed for specific treatment.

Within the health center, the results of pamphlet distribution can already be seen in the increased awareness and responsiveness of employees to a patient's rights. The hope is that through publication and dissemination of "Your Rights as a Patient," patients will begin to demand and receive their newly recognized rights at other institutions.

We have been delighted to see our patients' manual returned to us under the name and banner of other health care institutions. Those who share our values and goals have adopted and adapted some of our approaches for their own specific circumstances. Mutual borrowing and the exchange of ideas and policies to further advance the recognition of patients' rights will significantly contribute to the assurance of quality health care.

6

History of the Problem-Oriented Medical Record Audit

William B. Lloyd, M.D.

The keeping of good, communicative patient records was an important goal from the beginning of the center. Efficient communication among team members demanded standardized legible charts. At that time, Dr. Lawrence Weed's new concept of a problem-oriented medical record was being widely discussed. Consequently, he was invited to speak to the entire staff on the method and its advantages. Significant enthusiasm for the method developed following his visit in August 1968. Shortly thereafter, it became medical department policy to keep a problem list on each record. Many practitioners adopted the method in whole or in part.

The original problem list was subsequently modified by printing "Health Maintenance" as problem number one on problem lists before they were placed in the medical record. This adaptation of the POMR method emphasized the high priority placed upon health maintenance among the overall goals of health care provided by the agency.

Despite this early interest in the POMR method, acceptance by practitioners was slow. Most of those practitioners who did adopt the method did so only in part or used it incorrectly. Therefore, in 1973, a major developmental effort to adapt the POMR method to the Dr. Martin Luther King Jr. Health Center setting and to educate practitioners in its use was undertaken.

Dr. John Alcott, one of our social medicine residents,

directed and inspired the preparation of a new problem list and a booklet explaining in considerable detail the use of the revised method. The booklet was finished in May 1974 and was distributed to practitioners and discussed in each practitioner group during the following months (see Appendix A for the POMR Manual). To remove any uncertainty about the administration's commitment to the use of the POMR, the director of health services informed all practitioners in a memo on June 19, 1974, that the use of the method had been made departmental policy and that an audit program to monitor adherence to the method would be developed effective July 1, 1974.

The idea of developing a clerical audit to monitor adherence to the POMR method was proposed by Dr. Alcott when the methodology was developed. A major stimulus for the administrative support required to develop the audit was the hope that it would be the first of a series of objective audits of the quality of care rendered by practitioners which would be used along with productivity measures for salary determinations by the administration. Therefore, a quick unambiguous clerical audit performed on several hundred patient encounters of each practitioner annually to eliminate random variation was developed by Dr. Richard Bernstein. The original audit form consisted of only three yes/no questions (see pages 50 and 51). The three questions were weighted to give a total score of 10 points for each note audited.

Score

1. Are all problems on the problem list including health maintenance dated?   2

2. Does the most recent progress note (by practitioner being reviewed) have each problem preceded by a problem title?   4

3. Does that progress note have all problems written with SOAP format, that is, does each problem discussed have the letters *S, O, A,* and *P* following it?   <u>4</u>

    Total   10

Performance of the audit was decentralized to the units. A simple check list was developed for use by the unit manager to monitor the performance of the audit by medical assistants (see page 51). It was anticipated that if each medical assistant audited progress notes of six patient encounters per week, each team practitioner would have between two and three hundred notes audited per year. The design of the audit was kept simple. No more than thirty seconds were required for performance of the audit on the chart and progress note. Thus the procedure did not impose an excessive burden on the medical assistants. One session per week was chosen for each practitioner and the charts of all patients seen by that practitioner were audited. Tight supervisory controls were developed. The unit manager monitored a certain number of audits performed by each assistant on his or her unit and the director of health services periodically compared the medical assistant's audit, the unit manager's review, and the actual chart.

Results

The outcome of the POMR audit has been very positive. The initial projections about the number of charts which would be audited and the ability of medical assistants to perform the audit without interfering with their other duties have been borne out.

The major problem has been inaccuracies in the audit, that is, misinterpretations or misunderstandings by medical assistants of the practitioners' progress notes. Unanticipated practitioner idiosyncrasies were discovered for which the medical assistant had not been trained. Note, for example, the progress note of an MLK practitioner reproduced on page 50 (top). This practitioner has developed a two dimensional charting method which embodies the principle of SOAP below each problem title. This variation was ruled acceptable.

Some medical assistants misunderstood a basic feature of the audit and therefore performed it incorrectly. For example, some medical assistants were auditing randomly any note appearing in the medical record after July 1, 1974,

Continuation Sheet   Date: 4/11/75

#1 Hypertension	#2 Obesity	#5 Knee pains (arthritis)
S) Needs Aldactone	Gaining wt.	Needs APC with codeine
O) BP 140/106 Heart & lungs—nl	Wt. 218 3/4	——
A) Could be better	Worse	Stable
P) HCTZ 50 mg, ⁒ q.d. #30, X 1 Return to clinic 3 wks.	1000 cal. diet	APC with co- deine, #30, X 1

Simple Clerical Audit for Problem
Orientation of Medical Records

Clerical audit of the problem-oriented medical record (POMR) is a brief review of practitioners' charts, which is conducted by medical assistants on each unit and supervised by unit managers. The clerical audit involves the following steps:

1. The medical assistant reviews patients' charts which contain a progress note and the problem list, the medical assistant answers the three questions on the POMR Evaluation (see page 51). This process takes no more than a minute.
2. The audit is then given to the unit manager for scoring. (Question #1: Yes = 2, No = 0; Question #2: Yes = 4, No = 0; Question #3: Yes = 4, No = 0.)
3. Unit managers keep all scored audit sheets and are responsible for insuring that all medical assistants do five (5) audits per week and that each M.D. and R.N. get between three (3) and four (4) of his or her charts audited per week. (See page 51 for format for recording this information.)
4. The average score per chart on each practitioner (M.D. or R.N.) will be calculated by the unit manager on a quarterly basis. (When the system first began, however, scores were tabulated for the first month.) Each practitioner will be informed of his or her average score. If anyone's average is less than 4.0, he or she should be offered additional training in the POMR. If practitioners wish, they can be referred to the senior family health worker on the team or her representative for such training.

Figure 6.1

POMR EVALUATION

CODE

Chart Number Reviewed_____   ____

Physician/PHN_____   ____

Date of most recent
MD/PHN visit_____   ____

Reviewer_____   ____

Date of review_____   ____

1. Are all problems including health maintenance dated?   Yes/No_____   ____

2. Does the most recent progress note (by practitioner
    being reviewed) have each problem preceded by a
    problem title?   Yes/No_____   ____

3. Does that progress note have all problems written with
    SOAP format?   Yes/No_____   ____
****

FORMAT FOR UNIT MANAGER'S SUMMARY OF CLERICAL AUDIT DATA

Score goes in boxes

	1	2	3	4	5	6	7	8	9	10	11	12	13	14	15	16	17	18	Average
M.D.-A	0	4	4	6	8	10	8	4	6	6	4	10	10	0	6	2	8	10	6.4
M.D.-B																			
M.D.-C																			

ETC.

	1	2	3	4	5	6	7	8	9	10	11	12	13	14	15	16	17	18	Average
R.N.-A																			
R.N.-B																			
R.N.-C																			

ETC.

X=completed audit.

	1	2	3	4	5	6	7	8	9	10	11	12	13	14	15	16	17	18	19	20	21	22	23	24
M.A.-A	x	x	x	x	x	x	x																	
M.A.-B	X	X	X	X	X																			
M.A.-C	X	X																						

ETC.

including emergency room notes written by another practitioner. Such misunderstandings were quickly clarified with all medical assistants.

Sorting out these and other problems of the medical assistants and unit managers meant that almost one year was required before we were confident that the audit was being performed accurately. Positive changes in practitioner behavior became readily apparent as the audit continued. The average scores of all team practitioners went from 7.8 in July 1974 to 9.1 by December 1975.

Team internist	7.7 to 9.1
Team pediatrician	8.2 to 9.6
Internist housestaff	8.4 to 9.6
Pediatric housestaff	7.2 to 9.0
Family practice housestaff	6.5 to 8.4
Nurse practitioners	8.0 to 8.8

With many of the full time practitioners now scoring 9.0 on their monthly audits, the unit managers have been instructed to reduce the number of charts audited for practitioners averaging more than 9.0.

We draw three primary conclusions from our experience with the POMR audit.

1. Medical assistants can do clerical audits of practitioner charts if the task is defined clearly enough.
2. Practitioner behavior, when being monitored, can change in the direction of the desired behavior. This improvement in scores suggests that:
   a. charts have more dates on the problem list titles (contents can be more readily found in the chart);
   b. the most recent notes have clear titles so that it is easier to find on any one page the specific problem one is reviewing; and
   c. that each problem on each note has the letters *S,O,A,* and *P* written under it in some fashion, thus hopefully making the thinking processes of the practitioner more clearly discernible.

3. When practitioners start being monitored, they quickly raise numerous pertinent questions about the process.

One of these perplexing pertinent questions is whether the three questions listed above and their point values truly represent what is important in maintaining an orderly, easily understandable chart. Specifically, many staff argued that the four point weight given to the question of whether all four letters, *S, O, A,* and *P* are written under each problem described in the encounter note was inappropriately overweighted. They question why one must write down the letter *O,* for example, if there is no objective data to be recorded for that specific problem. Others think the dating of the problem list is much more important and think it should have a higher score than the two points assigned to it. Furthermore, the three monitored questions never point out if a problem discussed is even listed on the problem list. In other words, they do not assess if the problems on the progress note correspond with the problems on the problem list.

Because of these criticisms, the committee has reanalyzed the relation of the POMR audit to the quality of chart maintenance and has decided on the following five questions and scoring system:

	New Scoring	*Old Scoring*
1. Are all problems on the problem list including health maintenance dated?	2.5	2
2. Does the most recent progress note (by practitioner being reviewed) have each problem preceded by a problem title?	2	4
3. Does the progress note have all problems written with SOAP format, i.e., does each problem have the SOAP letter following it?	2	4

4. Is each problem discussed in the
    progress note listed on the prob-
    lem list?   2.5   —
5. Does the problem number in
    the progress note correspond to
    the problem number on the
    problem list?   1   =
    Total   10   10

Hopefully, these five questions and their relative values more directly reflect what the HCEC considers important in the maintenance of an orderly chart. Even with a high score on these five questions the chart still may not be totally understandable. For example, the questions do not monitor the legibility of the notes. (This is done in the comprehensive family audits.) They also have nothing to do with content. A practitioner's thoughts may still be confusing even when written as directed. At least, however, it will be more obvious with this system that the confusion is one of thought rather than of writing style.

The most serious argument against emphasis on the above system is that success in chart order and maintenance may not reflect a practitioner's ability to deliver high quality care. For example, one practitioner whose POMR audits are consistently poor claims that his population of hypertensives have the best controlled blood pressures in the center. Although untested, his assertion may be correct. Nonetheless, the HCEC still contends that an orderly, understandable chart, which we feel this POMR audit encourages, can and should be a goal in itself. If the above physician leaves, the next physician should be able to learn easily from the experiences recorded in the charts. Significant disarray within a chart may make reading it so difficult that another practitioner may have to discard it and start anew. The HCEC can not condone such behavior. In fact, HCEC encourages the opposite, better communication, through the POMR audit.

If the POMR audit is considered valuable, how should practitioner scores be used? If used to calculate pay raises, what percentage of a raise should be delegated to the keeping of orderly charts as opposed to number of patients seen per unit time, or to quality of care by outcome standards, or to diagnostic acumen, or to high praise in patient questionnaires? What is an intolerably low score, persistence in which might result in punitive corrective pressure? The difficulty of answering these questions has stymied our attempt to tie POMR scores to pay increases. Nonetheless, as shown above, the point scores, and presumably the charts, seem to get better. If this continues, monitoring and periodically publishing results may be the only motivating force necessary.

7

Disease Specific Audit Case History: Gonorrhea

Donald A. Smith, M.D.

In 1971 a resident in the Montefiore Residency Program in Social Medicine began practicing ambulatory care at the Dr. Martin Luther King Jr. Health Center. He had little experience with the out-patient treatment of venereal disease. Faced with numerous rapidly changing treatment schedules for both gonorrhea and syphilis, the resident undertook to write a treatment schedule for both diseases for his personal use. It rapidly became apparent, however, that there was confusion both among the permanent health center staff and among the emergency room moonlighting staff about appropriate doses of antibiotics for gonorrhea and syphilis, as well as about the interpretation of such tests as VDRL's and FTA's. Further-more, the methodology for obtaining certain lab tests and for the follow-up of treated cases was unclear. Finally, reporting of cases to the New York City Health Department was minimal.

To clarify some of the issues surrounding venereal disease, a committee was formed consisting of one member from all groups who had anything to do with VD: nurse practitioners; family health workers; and personnel from medical records, laboratory, pharmacy, central supply, emergency room, and central administration. A representative from the local branch of the New York City Health Department's Social Hygiene Clinic was invited and attended.

Weekly meetings over the next eight months accomplished numerous tasks.

1. Diagnostic and treatment schedules for gonorrhea and
    syphilis were written and approved by the physician
    groups.
2. Better liaison with the health department was made
    in the following areas:
    a. supply and pick up of city-supplied gonorrhea
        culture media was established;
    b. methodology for taking gonorrhea cultures was
        tightened to avoid large numbers of fungally con-
        taminated cultures;
    c. better utilization of city social hygiene clinic con-
        sultative and specialty services (e.g. dark screen
        examination of genital ulcers) was established;
    d. reporting procedures for cases of VD were estab-
        lished;
    e. responsibility for follow-up of VD contacts was
        shared between MLK and the health department.
3. A screening program for gonorrhea in all sexually
    active women up to 55 years of age was added to the
    routine Pap smear screening program.
4. An education pamphlet on VD written in the ter-
    minology of the community and printed in both
    Spanish and English was prepared.
5. Responsibilities of physicians, nurse practitioners,
    family health workers, and the lab were clearly defined.
6. A team-by-team educational program was completed
    explaining treatment schedules, personnel respon-
    sibilities, and disease pathophysiology. Health depart-
    ment employees taught MLK staff techniques for
    follow up of contacts.
7. Moonlighting staff were informed about new treat-
    ment schedules and required to conform to them.

The final step was to perform chart audits to see what effect this whole process had on practitioner behavior. The resident physician and Maria Uribelarrea, the nurse practitioner on
the VD committee, set up an almost weekly chart audit of
gonorrhea cases seen at MLK. A score form was developed for
use on each chart studied (see Figure 7.1). The charts of

Figure 7.1

GONORRHEA REVIEW FORM

Date of Review_____
Reviewer_____
Results of Review_____

PATIENT'S NAME_____

PATIENT'S NO._____ AGE_____ M_____ F_____

PRACTITIONER_____

DATE OF PTS. ENCOUNTER_____ SITE: E.R._____ UNIT_____

REASON FOR ENCOUNTER: symptomatic_____ screening f/u_____ contact____
other_____

Score Points	DIAGNOSIS	YES	NO	INDET.	RESULTS	POS.	NEG.	INDET.
1	Smear done?							
	Culture sent? (#sent)							
1	VDRL requested?							
	Wet prep requested?							

Score Points	TREATMENT DRUG		DOSE	Benemid given			Disp. for VDRL 4 mos.		
1				yes	no	ind.	yes	no	ind.
	Procaine penicillin								
	Spectinomycin								
	Ampicillin								
	Tetracycline								
	Erythromycin								
	Other_____								

1 EDUCATION
Indication of Literature given? yes_____ no_____ indet._____

1 FOLLOW UP
F/U for 1 wk. given for females? yes_____ no_____ indet._____
F/U to whom? Team_____ Health Dept._____ Other_____
Record of actual F/U at MLK? yes_____ no_____
Result of F/U cultures? pos._____ neg._____ indet._____
Medication given for re-Rx of positive?_____

Score Points	CONTACTS	YES	NO	INDET.
1	Evid. of attempt to elicit contacts?			
	Names of contacts in chart? (indicate #)			
	Record of ER contacting appropriate health worker?			
	Any F/U note by appropriate team worker?			

COMMENTS

Total Possible Score

Males = 5

Females = 6

patients with positive gonorrhea smears or cultures found at least three weeks prior to the review were pulled from the names obtained from the lab's gonorrhea culture and smear records. The original goal was to obtain weekly five charts of people seen in the emergency room and five charts of people seen on the units. Charts were reviewed and a copy of the score sheet was sent to each practitioner, with discussion with reviewer if necessary.

The following point scores were possible:

Diagnostic:	*Point Value*
1. Were appropriate smears, cultures performed?	1
2. Was a VDRL (for syphilis) ordered?	1

Treatment:

3. Did treatment follow guidelines?	1

Education:

4. Did chart indicate that VD pamphlet was given?	1

Follow-up:

5. Was follow-up for women in one week made?	1

Contacts:

6. Was there a note concerning contacts on the encounter sheet?	1

The theoretical maximum attainable score for a practitioner seeing a female was six points and for a male five points (there was no routine follow-up of treated males).

The chart reviews made it apparent that the patient almost never saw only one practitioner. For example, a female with vaginal discharge may have had a negative smear for gonorrhea, a positive smear for trichomonas, been treated for trichomonas, but have a positive gonorrhea culture report returned to the nurse practitioner one week later. The initial practitioner got a score appropriate to the data when he saw the patient, and the subsequent nurse practitioner got a score for her handling of the follow-up positive culture. Family health workers were evaluated on their follow-up of contacts and educational efforts. Thus, one case with three practitioners involved may have yielded an actual maximum attainable score of ten points, four points for one practitioner and three points each for the other two.

Results

Eight chart review sessions were done over a period of sixteen weeks. Sixty different cases were audited. These sixty cases yielded evaluation of the personnel listed in Tables 7.1 and 7.2. In addition, five family health worker encounters involved five different family health workers.

Physicians had more items to be evaluated than nurse

TABLE 7.1
Fifty-eight Physician Encounters

Number of encounters	Number of physicians having this number of encounters	Total encounters
1	15	15
2	3	6
3	2	6
4	2	8
9	1	9
14	1	14
	24	58

TABLE 7.2
Twenty-one Nurse Practitioner Encounters

Number of encounters	Number of nurse practitioners having this number of encounters	Total encounters
1	7	7
2	3	6
3	1	3
5	1	5
	12	21

practitioners. Thus the actual mean maximum attainable score for physicians was 5.0; for nurse practitioners and family health workers it was 3.0. As shown in Figure 7.2, the percent attainment of the maximum attainable score slowly increased among physicians from 40 percent to 80 percent by the end of the sixteen week evaluation period. Nurse practitioner and family health worker scores were too erratic to show any definite trend, but averaged 66 percent with a range from 21 percent to 100 percent. The improvement among physicians at first resulted from correction of improper treatment schedules, but later reflected better education and follow-up of people with disease and better follow-up of contacts. Nurse practitioners may be more acutely aware of these aspects of treatment because of their training, which is why

Figure 7.2

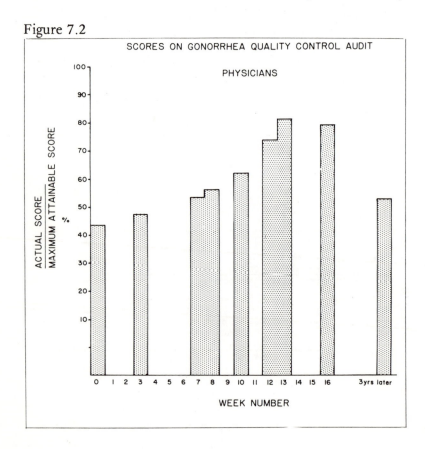

they maintained a higher score than physicians during the first half of the evaluation period.

A detailed attempt to determine whether the study reflected behavior change in treating patients as opposed to behavior change in chart recording was never made. In talking with individual practitioners, however, it seemed that each of the comments in the chart about patient education or follow-up contacts actually meant such items had been discussed with the patient.

The weekly gonorrheal chart audit was stopped after this sixteen week period for numerous reasons, principally because the physician and nurse involved became interested in other problems at MLK. The nurse has since left MLK to work elsewhere. The physician has remained, updating treatment schedules and procedures to reflect current trends. His title has changed from chairman of the MLK VD Committee to VD Committee Remnant.

In an attempt to see what effect the initial chart audit has had on a long term basis, twenty-eight charts of recent cases of gonorrhea were audited by the same physician using the same point system that had been used three years earlier. The twenty-eight charts provided a review of fourteen physicians having thirty-nine patient encounters. The physicians' mean maximum attainable score per encounter was 4.2. They attained an actual mean score of 2.3 (55 percent of the maximum attainable score). Nurse practitioners' and family health workers' mean maximum attainable score per encounter was 3.3. They attained an actual mean score of 2.1 (64 percent of the maximum attainable score).

This demonstrates fairly clearly that the physicians' scores have deteriorated from their 80 percent maximum attainable value which they reached at the end of the sixteen week audit period to a 55 percent figure three years later (see Figure 7.2). Nurse practitioners and family health workers have kept the same mean scores three years later (66 percent mean maximum attainable value then; 64 percent now). The change in physician scores probably results from the number of new physicians who weren't at MLK during the previous sixteen week audit period. Of the fourteen physicians currently reviewed, only three were at MLK during the previous chart audit. Their current mean score for three encounters is 67 percent of maximum attainable score as compared with 53 percent for the remaining eleven physicians. Of the six nurse practitioners and family health workers, only one is new. This group's score has remained the same over three years. The deterioration in physician scores has occurred even though the treatment schedules and procedures are still in use and new physicians are oriented to them. Most of the low scores are caused by the lack of patient education and inadequate follow-up of contacts. A few inadequate treatment and work-up plans still exist.

To effect permanent change in practitioner behavior, more than group procedural agreement is needed. A feedback loop of chart audit to encourage the new behavior is also required. If that loop does not exist, or if chart audit stops, an agency may never achieve the change or may slip back into old behavioral patterns. The regression from previous behavioral change described above was caused by an influx of new practitioners rather than by a regression in the behavior of those previously audited. Periodic reinforcement of the procedures with all practitioners involved and periodic reaudits are clearly indicated and will be instituted.

8

Comprehensive Family Care Audit

Donald A. Smith, M.D.
Gitanjali Mukerjee, M.D.

Comprehensive review of family charts has always been a central function of the Health Care Evaluation Committee. Initially, family chart review was performed weekly by members of the committee on one family chart pulled at random. Audited teams were rotated weekly to assure that each team was audited with the same frequency. A form for recording findings was devised. After the chart review, a member of the committee was designated to inform the team of the results at the weekly team meeting. Deadlines for performance of tasks overlooked in the giving of care were set so that the Health Care Evaluation Committee could reassess the chart in the future to insure that its recommendations were implemented. When the chief of a service felt that major errors had been made, he would personally discuss the issue with the practitioner involved. Although a possible fifty-two charts could be reviewed per year, only about forty-two were actually completed because of cancellation of health care evaluation meetings for various reasons.

Originally, the issues of audit involved the presence and maintenance of a problem list and gross errors of medical judgment. Numerous difficulties quickly became apparent. Because standards of health maintenance and disease management had not been agreed upon by group consent, irreconcilable differences of opinion on many issues often emerged. These differences created inordinate tension between chiefs of service and fellow practitioners, all of whom thought they were correct in their judgments. Additionally, although teams were supposed to be equally audited, some teams in reality were audited more than others, leading to cries of unfairness and favoritism. Furthermore, too few charts were audited to give a clear picture of how any individual practitioner was performing.

To cope with these problems, it was thought important to eliminate the conflict between the reviewing chief of service and the reviewed staff member. We believed that changes in practitioner behavior might be equally as impressive during the time the practitioner group was involved in determining quality standards as later when he was being reviewed. It was also thought that the responsibility of reviewing someone else would be at least as educational a role as being reviewed oneself.

Using these ideas as guidelines, the family chart audit was changed. First, over a one to two year period, group approved standards of care for health maintenance and common diseases were established by majority vote or consensus of the practitioners involved (see Appendixes C, D, and E). Individual authority was replaced by group consent. This eliminated numerous individual conflicts between reviewer and reviewed.

Second, teams were requested to review each other every month. The secretary for the HCEC would have a chart from each team pulled at random monthly. The eight teams were easily grouped into four pairs, since pairs of teams shared office space. Each team of a pair reviewed the other team's charts. Family folders for review had to contain at least one adult's chart and one child's chart, but no more than a total of six individual charts. The majority of the charts had to have one visit recorded in the previous twelve months. After completion of the review, the auditing team had to talk with members of the audited team about their findings. The report had to be agreed to by both auditing and audited teams. It was then returned to the HCEC for final review by chiefs of service on the committee. Comments or disagreements could be sent to either auditing or audited team. The results of the audit were then filed under each practitioner audited, and a copy was placed in the patient's chart for future reference by the practitioner on items that had been discussed.

When the new team-team audit was implemented, major problems arose. Among the first requiring a solution was how to teach teams to audit a chart, something they had never previously done. Standards for management of diseases and health maintenance had been agreed upon, but the old chart review form consisted mainly of spaces to comment about the conclusions of chart review, and did not assist with or standardize how to do the actual review. One member of the committee undertook to draft a standard protocol for chart review. It was presented to the committee, minor changes were made, and a new form was accepted for general use (see pages 70–82). A member of the committee was responsible for teaching each team how to use the new form.

Several important new features were added to the form. An area for initialing and dating the completion of each step was added to determine where the process was getting bogged down. A section for evaluating family health worker function was added. The major change was the addition of internal medicine and pediatric work sheets for the standardization of chart review for each chart. A check list for health maintenance features was provided so that each item had to be looked for to see if it had been completed. Furthermore, a problem list section required that for each problem mentioned in the chart, the auditor had to decide whether the problem was on the problem list, whether the data were adequate, whether the assessment was correct, and whether treatment follow-up was adequate. This feature of chart review reinforced the problem-oriented approach to record keeping. Demanding that such a detailed record of auditing decisions be kept made it easy for both reviewed and reviewers to see specific points of disagreement. Without such a detailed documentation, it was thought that chart review would degenerate into such meaningless generalized statements as "health maintenance generally good," or "care seems adequate," and the like.

Once the teams were taught how to review each other

using the new chart audit form, additional problems emerged. Teams demanded that time be set aside for chart review. This was denied by the administration on grounds of financial austerity. A huge delay soon developed in getting charts reviewed. Three months would pass without a team returning a reviewed record. Members of the slow team would accuse each other of the delay. To resolve this, a box was added alongside the name of each auditing team member to show when the chart had been given and when it was returned to the senior family health worker of the team. Once the delaying member was accurately identified, the chief of his service would talk with him to rectify the situation. At present, delays of over six weeks are rare.

When the new team-team process began, team members complained they didn't wish to audit their paired team because they worked so closely together that animosity created over audit of a colleague would be detrimental to smooth personal relations. This theoretical complaint was demonstrated by the apparent fact that the reviewing teams would not talk to reviewed teams before sending the chart to HCEC for final approval. The HCEC finally refused to review chart audits until reviewing and reviewed teams had spoken together. Slowly but surely this led to the hoped-for discussion between reviewer and reviewed. To date none of the anticipated animosity has appeared. On the contrary, there seems to be a growing understanding of the legitimacy of different points of view about how to handle health problems.

There have been many stimulating spinoffs from the team-team audit. It became obvious quickly that the FHW audit section of the family chart review was outdated. This resulted in an attempt to define the auditable components of the family health worker role. However, as yet we have not modified the audit form to reflect this clarification.

Often it was unclear where the boundary lay between a patient's and the team's responsibility for patient care. What was the responsibility of the practitioner at MLK for a complicated cancer patient being seen at Oncology Clinic at Montefiore Hospital? If a patient's hypertension was controlled, was it because the team was not aggressive enough to get the patient to return or because the patient was too unmotivated to return on his own, or both? Increased attempts to place responsibility on teams and practitioners were made which are slowly moving the health center toward a more aggressive stance as a health care provider. A hypertension surveillance project is now under way which will result in a more aggressive and more standardized approach to getting hypertensives to return for follow-up (see Chapter 9).

The detailed team-team audit soon led to the realization that although practitioner groups may vote to initiate new health maintenance procedures, e.g. tetanus-diphtheria immunization and stool testing for occult blood, individual practitioners are slow to add further levels of complexity to their health management behavior unless constantly prodded by such chart review. Such a simple procedure as tetanus-diphtheria immunization for adults, a task not taught by in-patient hospital training, has only slowly and painfully been instituted over a two year period by internists. This has been a direct result of chart audit.

The "Recommendations to the Agency" section of the form has resulted in one major change. Blood pressures were taken erratically in the emergency room/screening clinic and the specialty clinic, resulting in lack of continuity of care for this chronic problem. The recommendation for taking blood pressures on every emergency room and specialty clinic patient was made and instituted. This has lead to directing many hypertensives who casually use the emergency room toward more comprehensive health care supervision by the teams.

Continuous communication is maintained with staff about the quality of their audits, both to encourage compliance with procedures and to pinpoint gaps and inadequacies. Thus, when one practitioner repeatedly failed to record histories despite repeated reminders, he was informed that a specified number of his charts would be reviewed over a period of time and his further failure to comply could lead to his dismissal. The nursing staff, who consistently keep excellent records, are often complimented. Where a team does an outstanding job, they are similarly praised. Illegible handwriting, the bane of the whole procedure, is relentlessly pursued with each practitioner. The committee is not rigid when it meets resistance and makes every effort to communicate and to revise procedures to meet realistic needs and problems, but it is insistent that once a procedure is agreed upon, it be scrupulously followed.

Team-team chart audit has been slow and difficult. It asks hard working practitioners to find time to perform yet another task. The HCEC and its chiefs of service spend much time reviewing chart reviews of teams. But the process has made the health center more aware of its own behavior and of the need for change in many areas. Additionally, it has made practitioners aware of their strengths and weaknesses in health care. The institutionalization of the process as part of the every day operation of the health center will strengthen its function as the central core of quality audit by the HCEC.

Appendix:
Team-Team Comprehensive Family Care Audit

A. Instructions for Total Process

When the center's patient population increased and new practitioners joined our staff, the Health Care Evaluation Committee decided that chart review had to be done in a different manner. The committee thought that the individual teams should be more involved in chart review because it is an excellent training tool and educational experience. This new method would also help us to achieve our ultimate goal—better patient care. Therefore, the following criteria were established by the HCEC.

1. Charts are reviewed on a unit basis: That is, Team A will review Team B and vice versa; Team C will review Team D and vice versa.
2. The audit form is submitted in typewritten form. (See forms, pages 77–82.)

3. The chart for review is pulled at random two weeks ahead of time and handed over to the team for review.

After review, the audit form is submitted by the reviewing team to the reviewed team with pertinent recommendations. After applicable and acceptable alterations and corrections are made, the audit form is submitted to the chairman of HCEC. The HCEC reviews the audit, arbitrates on differences between reviewer and reviewed, and passes on to management any administrative changes suggested by the review. Any matter pertaining to the performance of an individual practitioner is reviewed by the chief of service with the individual concerned.

4. If the chart pulled has less than four individuals in the folder, a second chart is pulled for review; or if a chart of a family that has moved away is pulled, a second chart will be pulled for review. Charts pulled at random should be those of patients who are actively being seen at the center and who have been registered longer than one year. The purpose of the review is to audit team performance, so all members of the team should have an input.

B. Family Audit Form Instructions

The new form for family audit consists of three sections:

1. Family Audit Form, Health Care Evaluation: a four-page form to summarize findings on the entire family folder, pp. 77–80.
2. Adult Chart Review: a one-page work sheet for each adult's chart in the family, p. 81.
3. Pediatric Chart Review: a one-page chart sheet for each child's chart in the family, p. 82.

Instructions for each of these three sections follows:

Section I: Family Audit Form, Health Care Evaluation (See page 77.)

The person on the team who is coordinating the review

will be responsible for completing this form. All comments on this form must be typed.

The items in the first section are self-explanatory. The reviewing team must have an internist, pediatrician, nurse practitioner, and family health worker involved in the review. Their names and their team name (for example, Team C) should be written under the "Reviewing Team." Team name and name of internist, pediatrician, nurse practitioner, family health worker, and specialist (for example, Ob/Gyn) responsible for care on the reviewed family should be indicated under "Reviewed Team." If several different practitioners in one practitioner category (like internists) are currently taking care of a family, they should all be indicated. Names of previous MLK practitioners involved should be indicated as well. In confusing cases, please underline the *one* practitioner that seems to be the current primary care practitioner. The columns "Date Rec" and "Date Ret" are the dates that charts are given and returned from individual team members performing the review. If there is an inordinate delay in finishing the review, the responsible party may be identified.

Please list family members in the space provided, for example:

01 John   M   33
02 Susan   F   32
03 John Jr.   M   6 mos.

The dates at the top right side of the first page are to be filled in and initialed by the person designated in the parenthesis below the line. These dates must be filled in sequentially in order that the whole process follow a standard plan. The process begins when the chart to be audited is received by the senior family health worker of the team doing the auditing. He or she places the date and his or her initials in the appropriate spaces. The whole process ends when the entire set of dates has been filled in and initialed. Please note that the reviewing team must discuss the chart with the reviewed team before sending the audit form to the Health Care Evaluation Committee.

The next section concerns the family folder and family folder forms. The family health worker participating in the chart review indicates by a check mark (✓) whether the items 1a-1e, 2, and 3 are present and adequate, present and inadequate, or absent. Spaces for comments are provided.

Any member of the team may comment on the legibility of any practitioner in the reviewed chart by noting the illegible practitioner's name and chart number in the appropriate space.

If a reviewing team member should find misfiled information in any chart, he or she should note the name and number of the misfiled patient and the chart number where the data was filed. He should then either correctly file the information himself or send it to medical records for refiling. There should be no delay in this process: whoever finds misfiled information should note it and immediately send it for refiling.

The comment section should contain all comments on the care given each individual member of the family. The reviewing team should agree on the individual family member summaries that are to be typed here. Completing this section might be as simple as having the secretary type verbatim the comments listed under "Overall Assessment" on the individual adult and pediatric chart review sheets.

As indicated on the form, comments should include:

1. Adequacy of health maintenance to date; tests needed to be done.
2. Use of problem-oriented notes and problem sheet; specific comments.
3. Disagreements concerning diagnoses, follow-ups (F/U's), and/or treatments.

An example might be:

(01)—Health maintenance: needs repeat Pap, Tine Test, Tetanus Shot.
Family planning, hepatomegaly not on problem list.

No indication of resolution on problem list for dysuria.

Disagree with diagnosis of diabetes, needs oral GTT to confirm this diagnosis.

(02)— Health maintenance: excellent.

Family planning needs to be included on problem list.

Why no involvement of FHW in this area?

According to Freis Criteria, this patient should be treated for hypertension.

(03)— Excellent care and use of chart; no comments.

If during the review, the reviewing team should come up with any suggestions concerning center procedures and how they might be improved, they should be typed in the section "Recommendation for Agency Change" and be referred to the director of professional affairs for consideration and possible implementation.

The Health Care Evaluation Committee will review all audits and place any comments to the reviewing or reviewed team on this page. The secretary of the committee will give these comments to the family health worker who did the review and who was reviewed. If the reviewed or reviewing teams have any questions concerning the HCEC comments, they should see the HCEC committee member indicated at the the bottom of the page.

All completed reviews will be filed in the HCEC office under the name of the team who was reviewed.

Sections II and III: Adult and Pediatric Chart Review Forms (See pages 81 and 82.)

These forms are the basic work sheets for review of individual charts. They may be written in longhand by the reviewer.

The Chart Review Form is divided into four sections: Patient-Reviewer Identification, Health Maintenance, Disease Management, and Overall Assessment.

Patient-Reviewer Identification. This section is self-explanatory. All blanks must be filled in. "Internist" and

"Pediatrician" refer to the practitioner(s) being reviewed. The reviewer's name should be placed after the word "Reviewer(s)."

The purpose of chart review is to review team care. Occasionally, however, patients are very difficult and are either a chronic "no-show" or use the ER most of the time. Please indicate by checking YES or NO whether the reviewed patient fits into either category.

Health Maintenance. The health maintenance section is a tally sheet to indicate whether specific requirements of health maintenance protocols have been followed. It can be filled in by any team member in chart review. Items that have been done can be so indicated by checking the "yes" box and placing in the box the most recent date when the test or procedure was performed. Space is available under "comments" for clarification, such as "Tine test ordered 3/10/73, but never read."

Disease Management. This part of the form will be completed by a physician or a nurse practitioner and physician. The reviewer places in the boxes labeled "Health Problems" the problems that are written on the problem sheet of the chart. For each of these problems he can then indicate by checking the "Y" (yes) column that the problem is on the problem list, and the "Y" or "N" column as to whether there is adequate data base, assessment, follow-up, and treatment. If any of these areas are inadequate, the reviewer must check "N" (no) and document his or her opinion by commenting in the adjacent free space. In reviewing a chart a physician may find that several problems have not been placed on the problem list. In this case he or she should write the problem in the health problem box and then check "N" underneath it, indicating that the problem was not listed on the problem list in the chart.

Overall Assessment. The physician uses this space for his overall assessment. It is here that the recommendations to the reviewed physician for improvement are made. Equally important, comments of praise for good care can be made here as well.

Comments should include:

1. Adequacy of health maintenance to date; tests needed to be done.
2. Use of problem-oriented notes and problem sheet; specific comments.
3. Disagreements concerning diagnosis, F/U, and/or treatment.

These comments in the "Overall Assessment" may be typed verbatim onto the Family Audit Form under the section "Review Summary of Individual Family Members." In discussing the chart review with the reviewed team, the reviewing team will use these work sheets to document their findings.

Figure 8.1

```
                        FAMILY AUDIT FORM

                    HEALTH CARE EVALUATION


        Family Name_____

        Family Number_____

                        Date of receipt of chart by F.H.W._____
                                                              (Sr.FHW)
                        Date of completion of review       _____
                                                              (Sr.FHW)
                        Date discussed with reviewed
                        team                               _____
                                                              (Sr.FHW)
                        Date received by HCE Committee      _____
                                                              (Secy HCE)
                        Date approved by HCE Committee      _____
                                                              (Chairman
                                                               HCE)
                        Date recommendation was given
                        to reviewing team                  _____
                                                              (Secy HCE)
                        Date recommendation  was given
                        to reviewed team                   _____
                                                              (Secy HCE)
```

Reviewed Team_____	Reviewing Team_____	Date Rec'd	Date Ret'd
INTERNIST(s)_____	INTERNIST(s)_____		
PEDIATRICIAN(s)_____	PEDIATRICIAN(s)_____		
NURSE PRACTITIONER(s)_____	NURSE PRACTITIONER(s)_____		
F.H.W.(s)_____	F.H.W.(s)_____		
OTHER_____	OTHER_____		

```
Family Tree

   #        Full Name           Sex       Age
```

Figure 8.1 (cont.)

Family Folder	Present Adequate	Present Inadequate	Absent	Comments
1. Family Structure Form				
a. Family Structure				
b. Living Quarters				
c. Economics				
d. List Soc. Probs.				
e. List Med. Probs.				
2. Problem List				
3. F/U of Problems				

Additional Comments:

Format and Legibility:
   A. Writing (note practitioner, chart)

   B. Misfiled information (misfiled name, #, chart # where misfiled)

   (Reviewer should place information into correct chart or send it
   to record room for re-filing).

Figure 8.1 (cont.)

Review Summary of Individual Family Members

      Comments on each family member should include:

      1. Adequacy of health maintenance to date; tests needed to be done.
      2. Use of problem oriented notes and problem sheet. Specific comments.
      3. Disagreements concerning diagnosis, F/U's and/or treatment.

Recommendation for agency change (to Director of Professional Affairs, Division of Health Services)

Figure 8.1 (cont.)

<u>Comments from the Health Care Evaluation</u>
<u>Committee</u>

Comments to Reviewed Team:

Comments to Reviewing Team:

If Reviewed or Reviewing team has questions about these comments, please contact :

Figure 8.1 (cont.)

ADULT CHART REVIEW

Patient_____   Internist_____

Patient #_____   Nurse Practitioner_____

Age_____   Sex_____   Date of Review_____

Unusually high # no shows? Yes____No____   Reviewer(s)_____
Unusually high # ER visits? Yes____No____
                                            Date of last clinic visit_____
HEALTH MAINTENANCE Signature of reviewed_____

	Adequately done YES (date)	NO (date)	COMMENTS	TESTS COMPLETED	YES (date)	NO (date)
PAST HISTORY				Chest x-ray		
				CBC		
				Sickle		
FAMILY HISTORY				Urinalysis		
				VDRL		
				Pertinent Chem.		
HABITS				PPD		
				Td Shot		
REVIEW OF SYSTEMS				Pap Smear NA		
				EKG NA		
				Flu Shot NA		
PHYSICAL EXAM				Stool Occult Blood Testing NA		

DISEASE MANAGEMENT

HEALTH PROBLEMS	ON PROBLEM LIST		ADEQUATE DATE BASE ASSESSMENT		ADEQUATE TREATMENT FOLLOW-UP		COMMENTS
	Y	N	Y	N	Y	N	
	Y	N	Y	N	Y	N	
	Y	N	Y	N	Y	N	
	Y	N	Y	N	Y	N	
	Y	N	Y	N	Y	N	
	Y	N	Y	N	Y	N	
	Y	N	Y	N	Y	N	
	Y	N	Y	N	Y	N	

OVERALL ASSESSMENT

Figure 8.1 (cont.)

PEDIATRIC CHART REVIEW

Patient_____   Pediatrician_____

Patient #_____   Nurse Practitioner_____

Birth date_____Age_____Sex_____   Date of Review_____

Unusually high # no shows? Yes____No_____   Reviewer(s)_____
Unusually high # ER visits? Yes____No_____
                                        Date of last clinic visit_____
                          HEALTH MAINTENANCE Signature of reviewed

	Adequately done Yes (date)	No (date)	COMMENTS	TESTS COMPLETED	YES (date)	NO (date)
INITIAL HISTORY				Head Circum($<$ 1 yr) \newline BP (q/y over 5)		
BIRTH HISTORY				HCT \newline Sickle Prep		
MILESTONE				Urine \newline Vision ($>$ 5 yrs.)		
FAMILY HISTORY				Audiometric ($>$ 5 yrs.) \newline OPV 1, 2, 3		
PAST MED. HISTORY				D.P.T. 1, 2, 3 \newline Rubella vaccine considered		
PHYSICAL EXAM				Measles vaccine		
GROWTH CHART				Tine Test		

DISEASE MANAGEMENT

HEALTH PROBLEMS	On Problem List		Adequate Data Base Assessment		Adequate Treatment Follow-up		COMMENTS
	Y	N	Y	N	Y	N	
	Y	N	Y	N	Y	N	
	Y	N	Y	N	Y	N	
	Y	N	Y	N	Y	N	
	Y	N	Y	N	Y	N	
	Y	N	Y	N	Y	N	
	Y	N	Y	N	Y	N	

OVERALL ASSESSMENT

9

Hypertension Surveillance System: An Outcome Approach

Donald A. Smith, M.D.
Peter L. Schnall, M.D.

Hypertension is a highly prevalent disease among the black and Puerto Rican lower income population served by the Dr. Martin Luther King Jr. Health Center. It is common in patients whose charts were randomly selected for auditing by the HCEC. On numerous occasions it was found that the blood pressure of a patient with hypertension was not adequately controlled. In many cases, it was difficult to determine the cause of this lack of control from individual chart review. Was it caused by noncompliance of the patient, a lack of aggressive management by the physician, poor access to care stemming from difficulties in the appointment system, or other factors? From conversations with physicians and family health workers it became clear they did not know which of their many patients with high blood pressure were controlled and which were not.

We elected to initiate a surveillance system which would focus on improving the outcome of the practitioner-patient, team-patient interaction as measured by improvement in blood pressure control. Blood pressure control would then serve as a marker to evaluate the effectiveness of teams in managing a common chronic disease. We also hoped that if teams were regularly presented with the results of how they were doing in comparison with other teams they would be stimulated to better control their own patients' high blood pressure. (Our "model" is a variant of the famous Hawthorne effect first noted by industrial sociologists: human activity under study tends to improve.)

Given this background, the hypertension project was developed in late 1974. The initial goals of the project were:

1. to screen charts of all adults to determine the percentage with hypertension;
2. to develop a simple manual surveillance system which would assist family health workers in follow-up and would generate a periodic report by teams and physicians on the status of blood pressure control in their hypertensive populations; and
3. to use these periodic reports as a stimulus to improve the care which the health center renders to hypertensive patients.

Identification of Patients with Hypertension

The first task was to identify patients with hypertension in the registered adult population. Each of the eight Martin Luther King health teams reviewed the charts of all adults listed on a computer printout in April 1975. Patients to be screened were:

a. over 19 years of age (born before 1956);
b. not pregnant; and
c. alive as of 10/1/75 and had made one visit to MLK since 9/15/73.

From the patients who fulfilled the above criteria, an individual was declared to have hypertension if:

a. he had a good history of hypertension and was currently on anti-hypertensive medication; or
b. was on no anti-hypertensives but had either a systolic or diastolic average on three consecutive blood pressures prior to 10/1/75 of —

age 20-49: systolic > 140 mm Hg or diastolic > 90 mm Hg
age 50 and over: systolic > 160 mm Hg or diastolic > 95 mm Hg

A person with only one or two blood pressures taken prior to 10/1/75 was also added if his individual blood pressure or average blood pressure was greater than the above limits.

As of this writing, all eight teams have completed the chart review. The findings are given in Table 9.1.

Table 9.1

	TEAM							
	A	B	C	D	E	F	G	H
Number of charts reviewed	N.A.	N.A.	N.A.	2129	2393	N.A.	N.A.	2540
Number of persons with hypertension	340	274	310	439	372	239	214	474
Percentage with hypertension	--	--	--	20.6	15.5	--	--	19.0

Three teams further clarified the status of their patients with high blood pressure by phoning, visiting, or writing a letter to those who had not been seen in the four months prior to 10/1/75. Patients were dropped from the active files for the following reasons:

1. Moved out of the MLK catchment area and using a health facility at a new location.
2. Disinterested in MLK, i.e., living within MLK catchment area but going to another health facility.
3. Misdiagnosed, i.e., displayed normal systolic and diastolic blood pressure on three consecutive patient visits while off anti-hypertensive medication.
4. Unable to contact, i.e., no response from any of the methods of patient contact.
5. Other, e.g., patient now living in nursing home and under its care.

The results for two teams of follow-up on patients not seen in the four months prior to 10/1/75 are shown in Table 9.2. Although an appallingly high percentage (48 to 60 percent) of registered patients with hypertension had not been seen in the previous four months, it quickly became obvious that our "active patient" list was outdated. A large number of these patients had moved, were going elsewhere, or had died.

Table 9.2
Initial Chart Review

	Team E	Team H
Number of charts reviewed	2393	2540
Number with hypertensive BP's	372 (15%)	474 (19%)
Number of hypertensives not seen in previous 4 months	225 (60%)	215 (48%)
Number removed from study by follow-up	74	82
Reasons for removal:		
Death	1	13
Moved	23	28
Disinterested or going elsewhere	16	24
Misdiagnosed	1	0
Unable to contact	33	14
Other	0	3
Final number analyzed	298	392

Surveillance of Hypertensive Population

Once we had identified patients with hypertension, the next task was to develop a system for surveillance. This system was intended to assist family health workers in follow-up of patients and to generate periodic reports to teams on how they were doing in controlling the blood pressures of their patients with hypertension. Although a computerized approach was explored, we found that a computer was simply not available to perform this task at this time. We also felt a simpler, inexpensive manual system would have more applicability to other practitioners than a complex expensive computerized program. Finally, we felt we could adapt to a computer later if the manual system became too cumbersome.

Consequently we developed a manual surveillance system using McBee cards. We named the system the Hypertension Surveillance System (HySS) with a specially designed McBee card, affectionately termed the HySS card, being the focal element. The principle of the McBee card is simple. Each item of information may be coded on the card by punching a hole for that piece of information on the periphery of the card. For instance, the HySS card of a Hispanic patient looks like this:

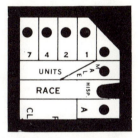

A non-Hispanic has a card that looks like this:

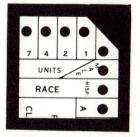

By putting a thin needle through this hole for ethnic background, Hispanics which have been punched as such will fall off the needle while cards of non-Hispanics will remain dangling on the needle. Thus the stack of cards representing Hispanics will be separated from those representing non-Hispanics and the number in each stack may be counted.

Instructions for preparing a HySS card may be found in Appendix F, and a completed sample card is shown in Figure 9.1.

88

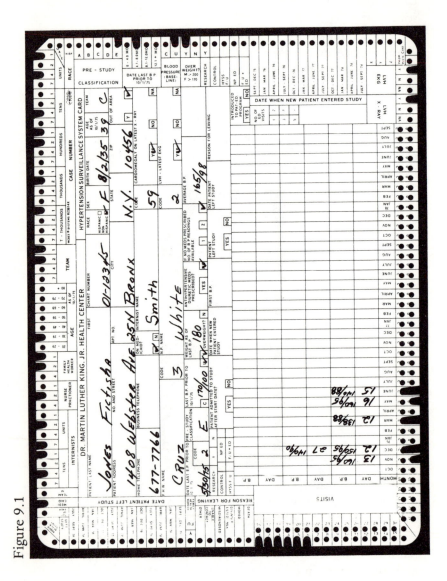

Figure 9.1

The crucial section of the HySS card for determining follow-up and for assessing the proportion of patient population under control for a given practitioner or team is the calendar section at the bottom of the card. It allows three entries per month and three years worth of follow-up before it must be replaced. Each time the patient is seen by a practitioner for hypertension, the card is pulled by the medical assistant from the HySS file, where the card is located sequentially by chart number. The practitioner records the date and the lowest resting, sitting blood pressure. The cards are collected during the day and punched "Controlled" (C) or "Uncontrolled" (U) by one specially trained medical assistant, secretary, or family health worker (called HySS operators). A patient is considered to have a controlled blood pressure if he is less than 50 years of age with a blood pressure $\leq 140/90$ or if he is 50 or over with a blood pressure $\leq 160/95$. The cards are then replaced in the file. At any point in time, one can locate and separate the cards for those patients seen in any one month and divide them according to whether they are controlled or uncontrolled. Since most patients with hypertension are given only three months supply of medication, those not seen within three months prior to analysis are selected for follow-up by family health workers on the assumption that they have run out of medication. The HySS card of such a patient is punched "Family Health Worker Follow-Up—Yes" on the left side of the card, is photostated for distribution to the family health worker, and is refiled in the active file.

Follow-up by family health workers follows a protocol (see Appendix F for details and standardized letters). For example, follow-up of a patient living in the MLK catchment area proceeds according to the following sequence until the patient comes for an appointment:

1. Telephone call.
2. Standard letter # 1.
3. Home visit.
4. Standard letter # 2 with a return reply postcard.

Notes about follow-up are recorded by FHW's on the xerox of the patient's HySS card and are reviewed with family health workers by the HySS operators. When the patient shows for an appointment, the HySS operator covers over the punch mark "Family Health Worker Follow-Up—Yes," refiles the card in the active file, and tells the family health worker that the patient has come in and the follow-up is complete.

A patient's HySS card is removed from the active file and no further follow-up is done if he falls into any of the categories previously listed: moved, disinterested, misdiagnosed, or unable to contact. A patient who has been contacted, given an appointment, and who said he would be coming but never showed up, is not removed from the active file on the first follow-up but is kept in the active file for follow-up for one year. If by then the FHW is unsuccessful in getting the patient in, the card will be removed from the active file and no further follow-up will be performed.

The date chosen for the inception of the study was October 1, 1975, at which time we began actively publicizing with the teams and the internist group that a hypertension study was beginning and that their results would be published periodically in the future. It was not until January 1976, however, that the HySS cards of three teams, Teams E, F, and H, were placed in operation. Plans are now being made to implement the HySS system on the remaining five teams in the summer of 1977.

The first data was analyzed for Teams E, F, and H in early 1977 and reports were sent back to those three teams in April 1977. The cohort of patients analyzed were those patients with hypertension who had remained in the active file after the first two month follow-up which ended December 1976. The number of patients finally analyzed may be seen in Table 9.2 for Teams E and H. Follow-up had not been completed in some cases by that time and thus each cohort contained some patients who were in fact inactive and have not been seen since 10/1/75.

Results

Table 9.3 shows the results by team for each quarter beginning 10/1/75 and ending 12/31/76. Section A shows that

TABLE 9.3
Team Results (Quarter Ending_____)

Team	Baseline 10/1/75	12/31/75	3/31/76	6/30/76	9/30/76	12/31/76	Number of patients (N)	Comparing 12/31/75 and 12/31/76 Z Value [a]	p
A. Percent of hypertensives seen in last 4 months									
E	68	75	70	68	67	62	298		
F	75	68	68	65	70	68	239		
H	70	74	79	76	69	69	392		
B. Percent of hypertensives controlled (total)									
E	57	61	66	71	75	77	298		
F	37	41	41	46	51	59	239		
H	39	41	46	54	53	55	392		
C. Percent of hypertensives controlled (patients seen in last 4 months)									
E	--	62	73	75	82	80	193,207, 203,199, 186.	7.82	<.01
F	--	49	50	54	53	60	144,159, 155,165, 163.	3.92	<.01
H	--	42	49	59	56	57	291,312, 292,270, 268.	7.14	<.01

[a] Z values for comparing proportional differences between percentage control at 12/31/75 and 12/31/76 on the same populations were calculated according to the formula:

$$z = \frac{(p_1 - p_2)}{\sqrt{\frac{pq}{n}}}.$$

Differences were significant at p = <.05 for Z values greater than 1.96.

between 62 and 79 percent of the total cohort of patients had been seen in four months prior to each quartile analysis. Stated another way, 21 to 38 percent of patients needed follow-up each quarter. Section B shows the percentage of the total original cohort with controlled blood pressure at the end of each quarter. Acute changes in team therapeutic behavior are probably best seen in Section C which analyzes the percentage of patients with controlled blood pressures seen in the four months prior to analysis. For example, Team E made major improvements in control in the first and third quarters of 1976, Team F in the second and fourth quarters of 1976, and Team H in the first and second quarters of 1976. The important point is that significant improvement has occurred over the 15 month period.

Since physicians are the primary source of care for hypertension on the three teams thus far analyzed, explanations for changes in team behavior might be found by looking at physician behavior. Table 9.4 shows how the three physicians on each team have done in terms of pressure control in their patients. Four of the nine physicians, representing 65 percent of patients being treated, significantly improved their percentage under control. E_1 improves from 59 to 83 percent; F_1 from 49 to 62 percent; F_2 from 48 to 64 percent; and H_1 from 40 to 60 percent. The patterns of change vary among physicians. For example, doctors E_1 and H_1 both made major improvements in control in the first six months of the study, whereas doctors F_1 and F_2 —and consequently their Team F— make their most significant improvement in the final quarter of the analysis.

Our first hypothesis to explain the improvement in hypertension control was that the patients with hypertension who showed improvement were visiting their physician more often. A look through a series of charts of patients with hypertension chosen randomly for four physicians, however, showed that although the mean number of patient visits per physician per quarter rose for some physicians, the increase in such visits did not completely correlate with improvement of blood pressure (Table 9.4).

One problem in interpreting our results emerged during

TABLE 9.4
Physician Results (Quarter Ending _____)

	Baseline 10/1/75	12/31/75	3/31/76	6/30/76	9/30/76	12/31/76	Number of Patients (N)	Comparing 12/31/75 and 12/31/76	
								z	p
Percent of hypertensives controlled (Patients seen in last 4 months)									
Dr. E1	--	59	75	80	83	83	118,122,120,122,114	5.33	<.01
E2	--	77	80	67	86	80	13,15,15,14,15	--	NS
E3[a]	--	65	69	68	79	72	62,70,68,63,57	1.64	NS
Dr. F1	--	49	54	56	56	62	47,59,54,55,52	2.6	<.01
F2	--	48	48	54	52	64	60,61,65,73,75	3.7	<.01
F3[a]	--	49	46	50	49	47	37,39,36,37,36	--	NS
Dr. H1	--	40	47	58	59	60	171,189,184,173,177	7.7	<.01
H2	--	43	44	55	48	47	96,100,88,80,78	1.1	NS
H3[a]	--	58	83	85	59	69	24,23,20,17,13	--	NS
Mean number of patient visits to physician in 3 – month period									
Dr. E1	--	0.9	1.1	1.2	1.2	1.3	32		
Dr. F2	--	1.3	1.0	1.2	1.2	1.3	30		
Dr. H1	--	1.2	1.3	1.1	1.0	1.4	45		
Dr. H2	--	1.2	1.2	1.3	1.3	1.6	31		

[a] Internal medicine residents.

the study when one physician stated that his technique for measuring blood pressure changed over the course of the analysis. Originally he took sitting, resting blood pressures. Subsequently he took standing, post-exercise blood pressures, which tended to be lower. Since he was instructed to report the lowest blood pressure at any one visit, he may have improved his results by utilizing this different way of taking pressure rather than by changing the actual pressures themselves.

No physician related the improvement in control to changes in their medication regimens, although charts have not yet been examined with this possibility in mind. We conclude that the institution of a monitoring system somehow initiated the change toward improved blood pressure control for our patients with hypertension. The specifics of this change have yet to be elucidated.

Just as intriguing as the changes in percentage of control over time is the variation among physicians in percentage of patients with pressures controlled at any one time. The percentage of control in the total cohort of patients with hypertension of each physician as of 12/31/76 is as follows:

Dr. E_1—79   Dr. F_1—59   Dr. H_1—59
Dr. E_2—74   Dr. F_2—64   Dr. H_2—47
Dr. E_3—71   Dr. F_3—54   Dr. H_3—66

Do these results reflect differences in patient population or differences in physicians and their approach to blood pressure control? Table 9.5 tabulates the differences in patient populations of the six physicians with patient populations of fifty or more, listed from left to right in descending order of percentage of patients with controlled pressures. The differences in percentage of patients controlled vary significantly among physicians, the greatest differences being represented by the physicians at the extremes of the gradient. Several demographic parameters in the patient populations vary significantly as well, including age, race, Medicaid status, and whether they reside in or out of the MLK catchment area.

It is known at MLK that Team E's patient population is

TABLE 9.5

	E1	E3	F2	F1	H1	H2	df	χ^2	p
Number of patients with hypertension	179	96	96	84	237	123			
Percent of total population controlled as of 12/31/76	79	71	64	59	59	47	5	37.0	<.001
Sex (percent):									
M	21	31	23	27	29	25	5	5.3	N.S.
F	79	69	77	73	71	75			
Age (percent):									
20-29	5 ⎫	7 ⎫	4 ⎫	1 ⎫	5 ⎫	6 ⎫			
30-39	17 ⎬ 46	21 ⎬ 46	6 ⎬ 36	17 ⎬ 32	8 ⎬ 32	12 ⎬ 42	5	12.6	<.05
40-49	24 ⎭	18 ⎭	26 ⎭	14 ⎭	19 ⎭	24 ⎭			
50-59	22	27	25	34	29	22			
60-69	17	15	24	20	23	19			
70-79	11	9	15	10	14	12			
80+	4	3	0	4	2	5			
Percent Hispanic	19	14	16	8	8	10	5	14.6	<.02
Percent on Medicaid	51	56	44	43	42	68	5	27.0	<.001
Percent out of area	6	8	21	8	19	23	5	29.2	<.001
Percent heart enlargement on EKG and/or x-ray	37	36	31	32	37	43	5	4.2	N.S.
Percent overweight (F>170 lbs.; M>200 lbs.)	49	38	45	51	39	41	5	8.0	N.S.

different from that on other teams. Team E's geographic catchment area includes mostly city housing projects, the most physically stable and generally desirable housing in the community, whereas other teams cover areas with fewer large housing projects and more walk-up tenements. With this in mind, we felt that perhaps Team E's patients might differ significantly from Team F and H's populations combined. When the comparison was made, shown in Table 9.6, it was found that Team E did have a higher percentage of patients with controlled blood pressures. In addition their population was also significantly younger, included more Hispanics, and tended to live in the MLK catchment area. This data is consistent with previously published data that older people have blood pressures that are more difficult to control than younger and that black people have a higher prevalence of severe hypertension as a group, they are much harder to bring under control as a group. The out-of-area/in-area difference has not yet been analyzed to see whether its association with control is independent of age and race.

The next question to be answered is what might be the maximum attainable percentage control for each population without causing deleterious side effects. As mentioned in Chapter 1, two-thirds of patients involved in the Model Cities Prepaid Health Care Project in Seattle had controlled pressures (*JAMA* 233:245, 1975). The Clinical Hypertension Center at Albert Einstein College of Medicine, which is part of the National Hypertension Detection and Follow-up Program, uses nurse practitioners to treat patients of a higher socioeconomic status than ours. Their results show about 80 to 85 percent of patients controlled at any one time (personal communication).

MLK physicians maintain from 47 to 80 percent control of their patients with hypertension. We hope that confirmed publication of these figures within MLK will further stimulate all physicians and teams to improve their results. At some point the agency will reach a plateau of blood pressure control which will better represent the limits of ambulatory intervention in the control of the hypertensive pandemic in similar communities.

TABLE 9.6
Patient Population Characteristics of Team E Compared with Teams F and H[a]

	Team E	Teams F and H	df	χ^2	p
Number of patients with hypertension	275	540			
Percent of population controlled as of 12/31/76	77	57	1	35.7	<.001
Percent in Age 20-49	46	35	1	8.7	<.01
Percent Hispanic	17	10	1	9.0	<.01
Percent out of area	7	18	1	17.5	<.001
Percent on Medicaid	53	49	1	1.3	N.S.

[a]Team E = Patients of Drs. E1 and E3

Team F = Patients of Drs. F1 and F2

Team H = Patients of Drs. H1 and H2

10

Dental Care Evaluation

Malvin F. Braverman, D.M.D.

Dental audit at the Dr. Martin Luther King Jr. Health Center began as a chart audit. Dental records were reviewed by the chief of dentistry at weekly Health Care Evaluation Committee meetings, along with the medical records of families chosen at random. This process continues to follow the chart evaluation protocol (see pages 100-103). Criteria were agreed upon by the practitioners to insure both quality treatment and uniform records. Uniform standards for recording examination findings and treatment planning are especially important where several practitioners may care for the same patient.

The chart evaluation criteria can be measured objectively by a check list for the presence or absence of adequate x-ray films, plaque control, scaling, prophylaxis and fluoride treatment, medical history, carious lesions, charting treatment plan, legible and complete notes, identifying patient information, and flow of work to be done at successive appointments. This phase of evaluation has proved useful. Having an organized plan and record results in complete dental treatment. The radiographs are checked against the charting for accuracy in recording of carious and missing teeth which require restoration.

Originally, chart audit was performed solely by the chief of dentistry. A further step has been taken by having dentists review each other's charts. This has resulted in a broader exposure to problem areas and has increased their awareness beyond their own records to those of their colleagues. They

Figure 10.1

```
                          CHART EVALUATION

NAME_____    RECORDERS_____

HOUSEHOLD #_____                _____

THERAPISTS_____                 _____

          _____

          _____


1.    TOP OF CHART - to include:  Name, Address, Household Numbers, 3rd Party Coverage,

      Phone Number, Birthdate.

                Complete_____

                Incomplete_____

                          (Responsibility - Receptionist)

2.    MEDICAL HISTORY

                Complete_____

                Incomplete_____

                Not Taken_____

                Consent signed when indicated_____

                          (Responsibility - Receptionist)

      Check if medical problem is considered in treatment (i.e. consultation, drug

      therapy, relation to dental problems)    Yes_____

                                               No_____

3.    PROBLEM LIST

                Complete_____

                Incomplete_____

                Absent_____

      Comments:_____

                _____

                _____

                          (Responsibility - Dentist)
```

Figure 10.1 (cont.)

4. CHARTING

A. Check the following for the initial charting

Complete_____

Incomplete_____

Not Done_____

B. Check the following for the charting of completed treatment

Complete_____

Incomplete_____

Not Done_____

C. RADIOGRAPHIC EVALUATION   CHARTED   NOT CHARTED
(If not applicable indicate N.A.)   (Indicate tooth #)

    A) Overhangs of 1 mm or more on
       amalgam restorations   _____   _____

    B) Open margins on crown   _____   _____

    C) Caries   _____   _____

D. Comments:_____

_____

_____

(Responsibility - Dentist)

5. TREATMENT PLAN

Easily Located   Yes_____   No_____

None_____

If complete, check the following:

Not logical_____

Logical services planned and outlined by treatment phase only

i.e., periodontal, operative_____

Logical services planned and outlined by more than treatment phase_____

_____

(Responsibility - Dentist)

Figure 10.1 (cont.)

All obvious work overlooked is unacceptable (uncharted caries, overlooked
periodontal problems)

Discussion_____

_____

Lacks a concept of total care (demonstrates an unawareness toward periodontal
disease, malocclusion, occlusal discrepancies, habits, growth and development,
etc.)

Discussion_____

_____

6.   CONTINUATION SHEET

Check if following information included:

	Always	Sometimes	Never
Date of each visit			
Progress notes complete			
Progress notes legible			
Work to be done next at following appointment			
Name of therapist			

(Responsibility - Therapist)

7.   PREVENTION

Check if following information included if indicated

Plaque control   Yes_____   No_____

Fluoride for children 12 and under   Yes_____   No_____

Scaling for adults   Yes_____   No_____

(Responsibility - Therapist)

8.   RADIOGRAPHS

Complete (minimum of 16 x-rays or

1 panoramic x-ray and 4 BW's)_____

Incomplete full mouth survey_____

Figure 10.1 (cont.)

```
            No full mouth survey_____

            Quality_____

                    _____

                    _____

                         Responsibility - Dental Auxiliary


General Assessment




Recommendations to Dentist




Recommendations to Professional Supervisor




Comments from Professional Supervisor to the reviewed or reviewing dentist.
```

Figure 10.2

```
                          CLINICAL EVALUATION

Name_____  Auditors 1._____

Household #_____        2._____  _____

Practitioners 1._____         3._____  _____

            2._____

            3._____

         GUIDELINES FOR EVALUATION OF CLINICAL WORK 3-6 MONTHS AFTER
                          TREATMENT COMPLETED


I.   TECHNICAL AREA

     1.  RADIOGRAPHIC EVALUATION -4          Adequate     Number Inadequate

         bite wings

         A)  Overhangs of 1 mm or more on
             amalgam restorations          _____      _____

         B)  Open margins on crowns        _____      ____  _____

         C)  Caries not removed unless chart
             indicates an indirect pulp cap _____     _____

     2.  CLINICAL EVALUATION                 Adequate     Number Inadequate

         A)  OPERATIVE AND CROWN AND BRIDGE

             1)  Marginal percolation of fillings _____   _____

             2)  Overhangs or poor contour of
                 fillings at the gingival margin  _____   _____

             3)  Premature occlusion with gross
                 facets - can be checked by
                 testing active mobility on
                 tapping                       _____      _____

             4)  Uneven marginal ridges or no
                 marginal ridges. (Irregular
                 tooth position will be taken
                 into consideration)          _____      _____
```

Figure 10.2 (cont.)

		Adequate	Number Inadequate
5)	Open contact areas excluding diastema	_____	_____
6)	Open margins on crowns	_____	_____
7)	Overcontouring of crowns on cervical area	_____	_____
8)	Poor hygiene qualities on bridges which includes		
	a) Improper embrasures	_____	_____
	b) Concavities on gingival surface or pontic resulting in inability to remove plaque	_____	_____
B) ENDONTICS		**Adequate**	**Number Inadequate**
1)	Apical third well sealed	_____	_____
C) PROSTHETICS		**Adequate**	**Number Inadequate**
1)	The partial frame doesn't seat properly - check patient's history as he may have distorted the partial or not worn it	_____	_____
2)	Abutments for the partial denture in poor periodontal condition (tooth in excessive mobility [2-3] with less than 1/2 the root in bone)	_____	_____
3)	Borders grossly over or under extended	_____	_____
4)	Poor occlusion causing skidding on denture base	_____	_____
5)	Flabby or irritated tissue underlying denture	_____	_____

Figure 10.2 (cont.)

	Adequate	Number Inadequate
6) Retromolar pad not covered by lower denture	_____	_____

D) PEDODONTICS

    1) Deciduous molars extracted without space maintenance is unacceptable unless orthodontics is considered or permanent tooth expected to erupt within 6 mos. of the extraction.

          Fabricated when indicated _____

          Not fabricated when indicated_____

          Fabricated but inadequate_____

II. PREVENTION AREA

    Use the modified plaque index to determine the efficacy of the plaque removal.

    0 - No stainable material observed after application of disclosing solution to tooth surface.

    1 - Discreet, discontinuous areas of stainable material observed on the tooth surface.

    2 - A continuous layer of thin stainable material at the area of the gingival margin.

    3 - A thick, continuous layer of material at the gingival margin, often covering half or more of the clinical crown.

Evaluate the Following Teeth	Plaque Score per tooth	Key for Index
1) Buccal 6⌋ or E⌋	_____	Up to 1 - good
2) Labial 1⌋ or A⌋	_____	1.1 - 2.0 - fair
3) Buccal ⌊5 or ⌊D	___ _____	2.1 - 3.0 - poor
4) Lingual 6̄⌋ or E⌋	_____ ____	
5) Labial ⌈1̄ or ⌈A	_____	
6) Buccal ⌈5 or ⌈D	_____	

    1) Evaluate each tooth above, if the tooth is missing, don't evaluate another tooth.

    2) Figure the average plaque index for the patient.

        a) add each score

        b) divide by the number of teeth evaluated

Figure 10.2 (cont.)

III. TREATMENT PLAN

    Discuss:

        1) Whether all oral problems were treated or mentioned in treatment plan (uncharted caries, and overlooked periodontal problems).

        _____

        _____

        2) Whether medical problems were integrated into treatment plan.

        _____

        _____

        3) Whether treatment plan logical and demonstrates a concept of total care.

        _____

IV. SUMMARY

    1. General Assessment

    II. Recommendations to Dentist

    III. Recommendations to Chief of Dentistry

review each other's records, and report discrepancies back to one another, and submit a copy of the chart evaluation to the dental chief. The review is then presented at the Health Care Evaluation Committee weekly meeting as a part of a family's comprehensive health care review.

Although a complete and thorough dental record is necessary for quality care, it is of limited use as an evaluation tool. The shortcomings of having only a record review are obvious. The dental record can reflect completeness of data, treatment planning, and adequacy of recording, but the radiographs are only objective documents in the chart that pertain directly to patient care. Everything else reflects the dentist's subjective evaluation. The dentist's thoroughness in the examination of the patient for caries, occlusal discrepancies, and soft tissue pathology is open to question with the best kept records. Also, a reviewer may know from the chart that a necessary prosthesis was delivered or a carious lesion was restored when needed, but cannot ascertain if it was done properly and is functioning well for the patient.

We, therefore, concluded that examination of the patient with the complete dental work was necessary for an adequate review of the quality of dental care received. A Dental Clinical Evaluation was initiated by the dentists (see pages 104–107). To increase objectivity, the dental coordinator suggested an external auditor. This immediately met with resistance from within the group. Why should we voluntarily open ourselves up to something like that? The memory of being a dental student abused by an abrasive and untactfully critical instructor immediately came to mind. Resentment toward the idea quickly followed, even though intellectually the group knew an outside evaluator would be more objective than an internal one, at least in the eyes of the general public. The idea was accepted when the criteria for evaluation were developed by the group itself. The auditor must follow a check list.

Other questions arose. Is an outside evaluator a "true peer?" Shouldn't a peer come from within the group? When the evaluator was chosen from a similar type health center this argument was overcome. A mutual audit system with a cooperating neighborhood health center in the New York area was set up.

The next questions raised by the staff dentists were: who will evaluate the evaluator and what will assure the quality of his assessment? It was decided that the MLK dental chief would perform this function by observing the auditor's examination and providing first hand feedback to the dentists.

Several patients of each dentist who have completed dental treatment within the last six months are chosen at random every six months. A clinical exam and chart evaluation are performed. The plaque index is measured on each patient being reviewed to determine the effectiveness of our prevention program. The Dental Clinical Evaluation thus consists of three basic areas:

1. Prevention, which measures the dentist's ability to motivate patients to care for their teeth;
2. Treatment plan, which reviews completeness of the therapeutic plan; and
3. Technical, which measures the technical performance of that plan.

A final summary is written which includes three parts "General Assessment," "Recommendations to the Dentist," and "Recommendations to the Chief of the Dentistry." It lists those dental problems overlooked, recurrent, or new to be attended to at the return visit. "Recommendations to the Chief of Dentistry" is reserved for corrections which are more serious and in need of immediate attention. These patients are called back to the subsequent peer review to insure adequate correction of these problems. Thus far, the complete Dental Clinic Evaluation has been performed four times, evaluating approximately twenty patients each time.

The following are some of the major conclusions of our peer review:

1. When the protocols are followed, correspondence between the record of treatment and the treatment provided is satisfactory.

2. Maintenance of the protocol helps minimize overlooking details of the treatment plan.
3. Failure to follow the protocol results in a confused record, and often necessary care is missed. This is especially true when preventive care is omitted which may result in recurrent caries.
4. Poor diagnosis results from incomplete and inadequate radiographs.
5. Health histories taken at initial contact become obsolete during extended treatment and require updating.
6. Patients seeing a dental specialist may require periodic referral back to the general dentist.

The peer review experience at our health center has been well accepted by patients and practitioners alike. The awareness of quality issues by the dentist has been increased, in some cases to an extent that he never expected. Patients view the added concern as an extra measure of the quality they have come to expect at the Dr. Martin Luther King Jr. Health Center.

11

An Outside Evaluation: The Morehead Report

Evaluation Unit, Department of Community Health,
Albert Einstein College of Medicine,
Mildred A. Morehead, M.D., M.P.H., Director

In 1968, 1971, and 1976 the Dr. Martin Luther King Jr. Health Center was evaluated by the Evaluation Unit of the Department of Community Medicine of the Albert Einstein College of Medicine. This evaluation was one of many health center evaluations funded by HEW and directed by Dr. Mildred Morehead. Under her leadership an evaluation unit was organized and visited the center for three days in April 1976. Each member of the unit specialized in some function of health center operation and explored in depth that function at MLK through interviews, medical records, and systems data review. The result was a 132-page document which not only described but also evaluated in detail the operation of the center.

The format for health care evaluation was standardized. Thus MLK could be compared with similar data from its own past evaluations and also from evaluations of other health centers. The purpose of including a verbatim report from the forty-page section on health care evaluation is to give the reader some comparative data with which to judge the quality of care at the center.

It was very heartening to hear that the care at the center could be considered "excellent." But when one reviews the chronic management data from individual cases one is appalled by the delays in diagnosis, the lack of follow-up, and the lack of appropriate referrals. These same problems came up constantly at the weekly Health Care Evaluation Committee meetings, and although similar criticisms are fed back to teams, one wonders whether this method can ever have significant impact in changing basic practitioner or team behavior. One can imagine that if the same evaluation were to be done five more years hence and the same systems for following chronic disease were still operative the results would be similar and just as upsetting.

One other failure of the report and of our own efforts at MLK is an inability to place the responsibility for what seems to be inadequate care. In the final analysis, the physician is responsible and most often receives contructive criticism. In some cases, nurse practitioners as well are subject to criticism when steps of protocol are missing. But family health worker activity, so far, defies scrutiny partly because their activities have been poorly defined, have often changed, and are so numerous as to be impossible to handle. Unless there are systems which give family health workers the capability of performing their responsibilities (e.g., getting the diabetic in who has not been seen in six months, refilling the INH for the patient who misses an appointment), we may be asking the impossible. If the family health worker has a system that tells her or him when the diabetic is overdue, then he or she can respond appropriately. But to be responsible for remembering who needs appointments for what for 400 families with no help to organize the information is a task no one on the team could possibly handle. Failure of this follow-up function is the theme of much of the criticism in the Morehead report. A focus on developing systems which will allow practitioners to carry out their follow-up responsibilities for their entire patient populations will probably improve care more than constant focus on individual responsibility in a series of individual cases.

What follows is the almost verbatim report of the Health Care Evaluation Unit. As the unit recognizes, review of small numbers of charts at one point in time has limitations when looking at total health center function. Nonetheless, the report has comparative value and the reader may draw his own conclusions.*

---

*The methodology of the Evaluation Unit is described in an article: "A Method of Evaluating and Improving the Quality of Medical Care," *American Journal of Public Health,* July 1956.

The Morehead Report
The Quality of Health Care at MLK

I. Method of Review

This review of the quality of medical care provided is based on an analysis of services provided in the fields of medicine, pediatrics, obstetrics and gynecology, and dental care.

A systematic review of charts selected from these specialties was made to determine the extent to which basic medical procedures appropriate to the age group and condition (pregnancy) were provided. Clinician specialists in internal medicine, pediatrics, obstetrics and gynecology reviewed other records selected on the basis of pathological diagnoses to assess whether clinical care was provided in accord with present-day standards of medical practice. In these reviews, emphasis was placed on the clinical judgment and performance of the attending physicians.

Built into the assessments are certain premises concerning the functioning of comprehensive group practice.

1. In group practice, even though physicians may as individuals provide good medical care, an acceptable quality of care from the standpoint of the group is attained only when the work of the group's members is so organized and integrated that the combined skills of the personal physicians, specialists, and ancillary personnel are freely available and efforts to alleviate patient problems, both social and medical, are coordinated into a team approach.

2. The method of organization should be such as to foster a closely knit relationship, with ongoing continuity, between the patient, his personal physician, and related team members. The personal physicians should assume the responsibility for coordinating the clinical findings of other specialists.

3. The center's responsibility for comprehensive care implies that responsibility will be assumed for total patient care and that administrative mechanisms will be established to facilitate coordination of care patients receive from all referral sources: backup hospitals, outside agencies, etc.

4. Each group has the responsibility to see that early in the course of contact between the patient and his personal physician, a baseline examination is performed which includes a comprehensive history and physical examination and minimum routine laboratory and x-ray examinations. These examinations should occur within the first three months after initial contact for adults and almost immediately for infants and pregnant women.

5. In addition to adequate clinical performance at an individual visit, the center has a responsibility for ongoing care for patients who use the center's facilities as their primary source of medical care.

6. Professional skills can become satisfactorily effective only when the medical record for each patient (and family) is sufficiently complete and organized so as to enable any professional in the center to obtain a clear picture from its study. This requires:

a. That a unit medical record be used and that fragmentation does not exist between different departments or providers of service.

b. That each record contains an acceptable history and physical examination and adequate data concerning the patient's social background.

c. That indicated progress notes be present and take cognizance of relevant changes and findings in the course of care.

d. That records include summaries of hospitalizations and reports on operative procedures and excised tissues.

e. That records include at least summaries from social service, mental health, and nursing.

f. That the medical record department be organized and sufficiently staffed to provide the essential support required to maintain this vital function.

7. The center has the responsibility to urge and educate patients to obtain medical services and to institute a rigorous follow-up system for patients with potentially serious illness. Special emphasis is required in programs serving the disadvan-

taged to assure that patients understand how to make the most effective use of health facilities.

8. Each center should have a plan for assuring that a high quality of service is provided. The responsibility for supervision and review of the quality of care should be clearly designated and actively implemented. Whether it rests on a committee, a department chief, or other professional individuals, ongoing review of care provided is essential to maintaining and improving the quality of service.

9. The goal of achieving a full-time core of dedicated physicians can be achieved more readily if a satisfactory professional environment exists. One aspect of this is recognition that a physician can maintain his efficiency only if his professional activities furnish him with a continuing medical education. It is the responsibility of the leaders of each center to organize and make available to all of its physicians and other personnel the unusually rich educational opportunities group practice offers.

The baseline studies were conducted on a series of random adult and pediatric charts and a group of records of recently delivered patients. This material was abstracted by center personnel and validated by the site team. A thorough and conscientious job had been done by the program staff. This material was submitted to a scoring process which enables comparisons to be made with other programs. These scores are based on an ideal of 100 points and percentages reflect the extent to which the ideal was achieved.

The clinical reviews were based on a series of records selected because the diagnoses indicated potentially serious pathology, conditions where medical judgment would indicate an appropriate course of action should be taken and where, in general, confirmatory evidence would be available from laboratory and x-ray findings. Each surveyor analyzed a series of charts and made judgments for each case in the areas of records, diagnostic management, treatment, and follow-up. A summary of each case was made emphasizing areas where deficiencies were found. Case summaries containing the basis for many of the recommendations were made available to the center but are not included in this book.

It should be stressed that many important areas related to the quality of medical care provided by the center are not covered in the following review and that the number of clinical cases reviewed was not large and possibly not reflective of total center performance. (Nevertheless, we hope that this review, performed by a group of experienced, well-qualified clinicians, will be of value to the center as it strives to provide comprehensive, high quality medical care to the residents of this depressed area of the city.) A comparison of the summary baseline medical care scores and clinical management scores observed at MLK and another 122 programs in the years 1968, 1971, and 1976 may be found in Tables 11.1 and 11.2. More detailed analysis of scores by clinical department follows.

II. Internal Medicine Services

A. *Adult Baseline Care (30 to 60 years of age)*

Names from computer printout of active registrants:

Percent of records obtained	100
Neighborhood Health Center Average	90
Percent of records meeting criteria of at least	
3 visits over at least a 3 month period of time	90
Neighborhood Health Center Average	60
Number abstracted	25
Male	2
Female	23

The retrieval rate was excellent. The percent meeting sample criteria and therefore receiving ongoing health care was well above the neighborhood health center average. The Bathgate Center, particularly, seemed to be regarded as the prime source of care for adult registrants between ages 30 and 65. The majority of this randomly selected sample were women indicating that the latter probably constitute the major section of the user population.

TABLE 11.1
Comparative Scores of Neighborhood Health Centers

A. Summary: Baseline Medical Care

Center	Date studied	Average	Medicine	Obstetrics	Pediatrics
NHC Average					
122 Programs		64	67	68	58
Martin Luther King	2/68	70	67	76	66
	4/71	75	74	79	72
	4/76	76	77	80	70

B. Adult Medicine: Components of Baseline Care

Center	Average	History	Physical Exam	Rectal/ Pelvic	Vital Signs	Lab x-ray	No. of Cases
NHC Average							
122 Programs	67	65	63	48	85	69	
Martin Luther King							
1968	67	41	77	50	50	85	17
1971	74	86	54	40	81	86	15
1976	77	82	71	51	87	81	25
Third Ave. Center	77	86	69	49	83	83	17
Bathgate Satellite	76	74	75	56	95	77	8

C. Pediatrics: Components of Baseline Care

Center	Average	History Physical	Measure- ments	Lab	Immuni- zations	TBC Screen	No. of Cases
NHC Average							
122 Programs	58	69	49	48	56	38	
Martin Luther King							
1968	66	71	37	64	76	76	21
1971	72	79	54	69	71	79	14
1976	70	80	56	74	71	46	27
Third Ave. Center	69	79	57	72	69	45	19
Bathgate Satellite	73	84	53	79	75	50	8

D. Obstetrics: Components of Baseline Care

Center	Average	Regis- tration	Prenatal Workup	Visits	Delivery records	Post- partum visits	Family plan- ning	No. of Cases
NHC Average								
122 Programs	68	32	72	76	57	59	66	
Martin Luther King								
1968	76	--	80	91	4	67	56	13
1971	79	38	82	91	63	77	69	13
1976	80	39	84	87	51	73	96	23
Third Ave. Center	80	40	84	83	47	76	93	15
Bathgate Satellite	81	38	83	94	59	67	100	8

TABLE 11.2
Clinical Management Scores

	1968	1971	1976 Third Avenue	1976 Bathgate	Neighborhood Health Center Average
Medicine	85	77	86	79	65
Pediatrics	71	80	87	90	69
Obstetrics	83	--	70	NA	73
Gynecology	62	--	80	NA	66

Health questionnaire in use   17

Adequacy of history:
Number of records with:
    Family history   15
    Past illness   19
    Cardiac review   20
    GI review   18
    Contraceptive advice   6
    GU review   22
    Social history   22
    Chief complaint and present illness   23
    Chief complaint only   2
Summaries of ratings for histories:
    Adequate (70 to 100 percent of points allotted) 19
    Fair (35 to 69 percent of points allotted)   4
    Poor (less than 25 percent of points allotted)   2

Health questionnaires were in use in many records. They were obtained by physicians and nursing staff. There was some effort to have those of the latter, which indicated positive responses, reviewed and elaborated upon by a physician; occasionally this did not occur, however. Some detailed social histories were taken by family health workers.

Adequacy of physical examinations:
Number of records with examination recorded for:
    Funduscopic   18
    Thyroid   19
    Heart   23
    Lungs   23
    Breasts   18
    Abdomen   24
    Rectal   9
    Vaginal   15 (23 ind)
    Reflexes   15
    Blood pressure   25
    Pulse rate   11

Weight	24
Height	18
Percent indicated only as "negative"	61

Time of most complete examination in relation
to first visit:

On first visit	12
Within 3 months	7
4 to 6 months	1
7 to 12 months	3
Over 1 year	1
No examination	0
Unknown	1

Summary of ratings of physical examinations:

Adequate (67 to 100 percent of points allotted)	12
Fair (25 to 66 percent of points allotted)	13
Poor (less than 25 percent of points allotted)	0

Physical examinations were, in many cases, not documented in a central location or at one time. Some of these findings were in the SOAP format, a rather "bits and pieces" approach fostered by the format which is inadequate if a complete initial assessment is not performed. This situation seemed to be less common at Bathgate.

A number of women were receiving care for family planning and gynecological problems and many were never provided with comprehensive examinations. On the other hand, some women with medical problems never were provided with pelvic assessments by their primary provider, nor was there any evidence of referral for routine screening to the nurse practitioners.

Vital signs and measurements were taken on most people with the chief exception of pulse rate.

Laboratory and x-ray studies:
Number of records with:

Hemoglobin, hematocrit	22
Urinalysis	24
Serology	21
Sickle cell preparation	12 (25 ind)

Chest film	23
EKG	5 (7 ind)
Pap smear	14 (23 ind)

Laboratory data base was a routine feature of care with few omissions, except for sickle cell and Pap smear screening procedures. One woman was referred by her primary provider for a Pap smear and never received it.

Positive tuberculin reactions were followed up by chest x-rays.

Average number of physicians seen for general care per patient	2.4
Average number of visits per patient	10.5

Continuity was fair at Third Avenue Center and good at Bathgate. Problem lists were used extensively with occasional slippage in maintenance. The SOAP format was also in abundant evidence. Flow sheets for monitoring blood pressure levels were found.

Hospital summaries were evident when patients were referred to backup institutions.

Home visits were made to several patients, mainly to follow up broken appointments by family health workers. Extensive nursing care was provided by referral to the VNA. There was no documented evidence of nutritional counseling or referrals apart from terse plans for types of diet.

B. *Clinical Management*

Fourteen charts of adults with significant disease were reviewed: eight from baseline audits, two from encounter cards, and four from the referral log. The overall quality of adult medical care was adequate and above the average seen in ambulatory care centers. The major deficiencies noted were in poor follow-up and/or control of disease and in delay in the diagnosis. An example of the latter was a 39-year-old woman who was first seen in the center in 1975. A fasting blood sugar of 179 was not commented on at this time, nor was a 2+ urine sugar noted one month later. It was not until eights months later that the abnormal blood sugar was noted.

In another case, a 52-year-old woman had diarrhea and vomiting several months after her first visit and at the screening clinic received B_{12} for the vomiting (this procedure was questioned by an auditor of the chart). Though there was some question of strong psychological overlay, a gastrointestinal workup was begun. The gallbladder series was normal. After several visits to the screening clinic over a period of six weeks, she became acutely ill and it was noted that she appeared to be in ketosis. She was admitted to the hospital and diabetic ketosis was confirmed. This diagnosis could have been made much sooner with routine blood analyses.

A 41-year-old woman was noted in the screening clinic to have a probable mass in her abdomen. Her hematocrit was 27, serum iron 27, and total iron-binding capacity 294, all of which were low. She did not tolerate oral iron and was given Imferon. She was not referred for the mass until two months after the mass was first noted at which time adenocarcinoma of the colon was diagnosed. Surrounding nodes were free of tumor. This two-month delay in referral was hazardous.

A 43-year-old woman was first seen in the center three years ago. In the subsequent two years she was treated only for obesity with diet and Tenuate (an appetite depressant). She did not maintain her diet and did not lose weight. Her first fasting blood sugar was 123; one year later it was 212; in 1975 it was 284; but it was not until seven months after that (two and a half years after her initial visit) that a 4+ urine glucose and a blood sugar of 485 were noted and diabetes diagnosed. During this time she had 17 center visits and was seen by 10 physicians who provided episodic care only. When she was finally picked up and followed by one physician, he was under the impression that she had received treatment for diabetes and hypertension in the past, which in fact she had not. He initially tried her on oral agents (known to be contraindicated in 1975) but rapidly found that her diabetes was not controlled. Insulin was then started; however, her diabetes was never controlled adequately. Her last blood sugar some months ago was 312.

Two patients had positive skin tests for tuberculosis about which no comment was made. Another patient, a 43-year-old woman, had calcium deposits in the left upper lung on a chest x-ray but no skin test for tuberculosis was performed. A 39-year-old woman had a positive skin test for tuberculosis and was started on INH chemoprophylaxis. There was a note in the chart saying that she was to continue this treatment for one year; however, there was no indication of renewal of her medication. A 52-year-old woman had a positive PPD. Her physician, however, failed to note that her initial PPD fourteen months earlier had been negative. This, therefore, was a conversion which represents a high risk of developing active tuberculosis. She was not given INH chemoprophylaxis.

In general, baseline examinations, including histories and physical examinations, as well as routine laboratory tests, were completed. There were, however, two individuals who failed to have a history taken and two who had no physical examination. Two also failed to have a chest x-ray and two failed to have VDRL's. Two of the ten women failed to have pelvic examinations and Pap smears. Thirteen were over the age of 40 years and six of these failed to have routine EKG's, three of whom also had hypertension.

Several patients had a number of screening clinic visits. For example, one had nine screening clinic visits out of thirty-two visits, another seven out of twenty-two, and another three out of three. In general, the continuity of physician care was good with the exception of the family practice team where only episodic care from a number of physicians appears to be given.

Nearly all physicians follow the modified Weed problem-oriented medical records system. Problems were listed on the problem sheet and/or progress notes with the subjective and objective findings, assessment, and plan of treatment for each problem. The progress notes were good and easy to follow. Though examples were given of poor follow-up of patients, many patients did have good follow-up and evidence of physician review of no-shows. The majority of women received Pap smears and gonorrheal cultures. One of the routine forms had a check box for indicating that the physician had taught the patient self-examination of the breasts. This item was frequently checked. In general, patients received appropriate treatment. In particular, antibiotics were used appropriately and tranquilizers were not overused.

It was clear from the charts that the public health nurses performed the pelvic examinations rather than the physicians. The work of the family health worker was impressive. Many of their notes were done in the SOAP form. Their instruction, given to patients with regard to disease and medication, was excellent.

C. Recommendations

1. The development of protocols for the management of a few more common diseases, including essential hypertension.

2. Reviewing and strengthening the computerized appointment system (though physicians are said to review charts of no-show patients for disposition, medical record audits suggest that a number of patients are lost to follow-up).

3. Developing better channels of communication regarding center policies, center meetings, and center activities with the Bathgate satellite facility.

4. Placing an adult physician on Team B who sees patients on a regular basis, to provide coordination for the patients seen by the family practice residents (apparently plans are in process for this physician).

5. Monitoring the center's policy of an EKG on individuals over 40 years and assuring that these are performed.

6. Reviewing and strengthening the policy for review of laboratory and x-ray reports, as a number are not picked up currently.

7. Improving the clinical management so that there is not an unacceptable delay in diagnosis.

8. Referring appropriate patients and family members to mental health as there is still evidence in the charts of inadequate mental health referral.

9. Noting positive skin tests for tuberculosis and assuring

that individuals at high risk of developing active tuberculosis (e.g., skin test conversions, young women who could become pregnant, patients on steroids, diabetics) are given INH chemoprophylaxis for one year (charts should indicate that medication is prescribed and taken for the year's period of time).

10. Consideration should be given to using nurse practitioners to a greater extent in the care of stable adult disease.

11. Summaries of team treatment plans should be in the medical records.

12. Team managers should receive training appropriate for the activities they are to carry out; however, limitations of these individuals should be recognized and they should not be asked to do things beyond their capabilities.

D. Summary

The overall adult medical care in the center is above the average seen in ambulatory care centers. Ratings for both clinical management and health assessments continue to be above the neighborhood health center average. The major weaknesses are related to occasional delay in diagnosis, poor control of common diseases, and loss of, or poor, follow-up. Generally, physician continuity is good. Routine histories, physical examinations, and laboratory tests are complete, and medical content of the progress notes is satisfactory. The activities of the family health workers are impressive particularly with regard to diabetic instruction. In summary, the overall adult medical management of the center appears to be strong.

III. Pediatric Services

A. Pediatric Baseline Care (Infants between the ages of 8 and 26 months)

Names from computer printout of active registrants:

Percent records retrieved	100
Neighborhood Health Center Average	91

Percent of records meeting criteria of
at least 3 visits over at least a 3 month
period of time 83
Neighborhood Health Center Average 62

Retrieval of records was excellent. As indicated by those meeting sample criteria, a high percent of infants are receiving ongoing care at the program, particularly at the Bathgate Center.

Number abstracted 27
Health questionnaire in use 2
Adequacy of History:
Number of records with:
Place of birth 22
Type of delivery 22
Birth weight 26
Condition at birth/Apgar 6
Family history 13
Feeding habits 26
Development 24
Past history 16 (19 ind)
Chief complaints only 1
Summary of ratings for histories:
Adequate (67 to 100 percent of points
allotted) 23
Fair (25 to 66 percent of points allotted) 3
Poor (0 to 24 percent of points allotted) 1

Health questionnaires were not found to be routinely used. A few records contained a checklist type of form which appeared to be a reminder of areas to cover without space for documenting information.

The lack of a questionnaire contributed to some extent to omissions in history taking, e.g., birth condition, family history. However, despite the lack of a central location or specific time for recording historical data, only one record contained no baseline data.

Adequacy of Physical Examination:
Number of records with examination recorded for:

Ear	27
Heart	27'
Lungs	27
Abdomen	27
Extremities	26

Percent indicated only as "negative"	60

Summary of ratings for physical examination

Adequate (60 to 100 percent of points allotted)	27
Fair (30 to 55 percent of points allotted)	0
Poor (0 to 25 percent of points allotted)	0

Most complete examination on

First visit	25
2-3 visits	2
4-6 visits	0
Later than sixth visit	0
No examination	0

Complete physical examinations were performed generally at the first visit. Abnormal findings were noted and followed up. Occluded ear canals were treated and reexamined.

Measurements

Growth grids present	yes
Routinely filled in	yes

Number of children seen in first year of life	27
No weights recorded	0
No lengths recorded	0
No head circumference recorded	3

Average number for children with recordings:

		NHC Average
Weights	4.5	5.3
Lengths	3.0	3.8
Head circumference	2.1	2.4'

Average number of visits:

first year	7.3	10.0

Number of children seen in second year of life	20	
No weights recorded	6	
No lengths recorded	8	
No head circumference recorded	17	
Average number for children with recordings:		
	NHC Average	
Weights	2.4	3.9
Lengths	1.8	3.4
Head circumference	1.3	1.0
Average number of visits		
second year	4.1	6.8

Growth grids were routinely used. Measurements in the first year of life were generally conscientiously and frequently performed, above the neighborhood health center average. In the second year of life, there was some slippage with a few more children with no recordings of growth measurements. The frequency of those with measurements was somewhat lower at Bathgate during this period than at Third Avenue.

Number of children with:	
Hemoglobin, hematocrit	25 (26 ind)
Sickle cell preparation	
Indicated	23
Performed	8
Urinalysis	18 (26 ind)
Tuberculin test	16
Percent of those tested with readings	
(Number)	63 (10)
Home visits	6

Basic laboratory studies were performed on many children. However, sickle cell screening was curiously infrequent considering the area being predominantly black and Puerto Rican.

Low hemoglobin levels were treated and repeated until improvement could be documented although one child, referred from a hospitalization with a suggestion that anemia be followed, failed to have a subsequent hematocrit. One child with a history of pica and plaster ingestion received KUB films but no lead level was reported.

Tuberculin testing was provided to a fair number of children with reasonably good documentation of results. A child with a history of INH therapy in its family was screened appropriately. This information was frequently buried in the progress notes.

A few home visits were made, mainly at Bathgate and mainly to follow up acute situations and broken appointments.

Immunizations:

DPT:	Completed 3 injections	23
	Completed 2 injections	2
	Received 1 injection	2
	Received no injections	0
Polio:	series of 3	23
	series of 2	2
	1 immunization	2
	no immunizations	0
Number of children over 12 months at time of review		23
Number with measles immunization		12 (23 ind)
Number of children over 15 months at time of review		23
	DPT booster	7 (14 ind)
	Polio booster	6 (14 ind)

Most records indicated a close adherence to an immunization schedule. There was some sloppy recording whereby dates of immunizations were recorded on flow sheets but not mentioned in progress notes or vice versa. One child at Bathgate was noted to have been receiving immunizations at Bronx-Lebanon; these were noted by check marks but no attempt to determine dates was apparent.

Continuity was quite poor at Third Avenue. The median number of providers per record was 6, with a range of 2 to 12. At Bathgate, the median was 2.5 with a range of 1 to 7.

Problem lists were maintained though with occasional

slippage, e.g., the child with a history of pica.

Referrals for hospitalizations were followed by hospital summaries in the records.

B. Clinical Management

The quality of pediatric care can be described as generally very good. The persistence in providing health care supervision to patients who missed many appointments is to be praised. Histories and physical examinations were generally quite complete. Heights and weights were regularly measured but head circumferences and fontanelle size were not consistently or repeatedly measured on all visits in children under a year of age. Growth charts were present in most charts and generally had multiple entries. Blood pressures were generally measured on school-age children but were glaringly absent in the case of the child with poor growth who later developed hematuria. Immunizations were generally successfully updated (even on episodic visits), although some patients still managed to elude the system.

Routine vision and hearing tests were generally performed but some detected deficiencies went without follow-up. Two children had positive sickle cell preparations included in their laboratory data but no note to that effect was in the record or on the problem list and hemoglobin electrophoreses were not ordered.

Progress notes were generally legible, appropriate, and in the problem-oriented format. Laboratory and x-ray reports were generally filed in chronological order. As noted above, however, some abnormalities went without notice or follow-up. Hospitalization notes were generally present but were quite confusing in the case of the child with abdominal abscesses post splenectomy because of duplication and jumbled chronological order. Hospital summaries were present to a greater degree than at most other family health centers. The results of some consultations were summarized by the primary physician when a formal consultation response was not available.

Diagnostic procedures in general were appropriate. Because the overall care was generally good, only minor criticisms can be made, such as the case of the two UGI series on a neurologically impaired boy with occasional postprandial vomiting in infancy; the use of such x-rays seemed excessive. Several urine cultures would also have been informative in trying to make a definitive diagnosis of a urinary tract infection. A child with initially unexplained tachypnea without pulmonary disease should have also had acidosis considered in the differential diagnosis of his problem. The child with enuresis should also have had a concentrated urine demonstrated in his assessment. In general, however, ill children were readily identified, the appropriate assessments initiated and the patient promptly hospitalized for more definitive assessment and therapy.

Consultants were generally used quite appropriately. Children with leukemia and Hodgkin's disease were managed quite well as were neurologically impaired children. A child with Down's syndrome and a VSD had apparently presented in congestive heart failure before consultation was obtained. Her nystagmus should have also been assessed by a neurologist. No result of a referral to ENT of a child with a hearing deficit was ever in the record.

Treatment showed no overt abuse of antibiotics. Most children with upper respiratory infections received throat cultures and symptomatic therapy but some did receive penicillin without cultures. One child was inexplicably treated with ampicillin for mild gastroenteritis. That child also received penicillin rather than ampicillin for an episode of otitis at an early age. In general, however, treatments were quite appropriate in specificity, dosage, and duration. Follow-up care was usually aggressive and well organized. Several patients were still successful in eluding follow-up.

Continuity of care was generally good for health care supervision appointments. Many episodic visits, however, were not to the primary care provider although this was not invariably the case. Even on episodic visits, there are numerous examples of provision of health care supervision and efforts to channel the patient back to the primary provider in an effort to provide preventive, continuous care.

In spite of the use of the problem-oriented record, some

problems (most notably positive sickle cell preparations and failed hearing screening) did not get listed and were apparently overlooked. Incomplete immunizations should be more often listed as a problem so as not to be overlooked.

The ratings for care to children were above the neighborhood health center average both in health maintenance for infants and clinical management of more seriously ill patients. The latter ratings were outstanding.

C. Recommendations

1. Greater emphasis should be placed on measuring head circumferences periodically during the first year of life.

2. Abnormal sickle cell preparations should be appropriately pursued with hemoglobin electrophoresis.

3. Even further emphasis should be placed on the appropriate roles of throat cultures in the assessment of pharyngitis.

4. Blood pressures should be recorded periodically on all children over two years of age.

5. Additional efforts should be made to bolster morale as well as productivity and to foster personal as well as professional satisfaction.

6. Reassessment should be made of the integration of the residents in the activities in the center. It seems they have solidarity and a sense of identity amongst themselves as a group but less so as integral staff members of the center.

7. An effort should be made to admit all MLK patients to those residents to further foster their team participation and provide more individualized continuity.

D. Summary

In summary, the pediatric service is a group of independent, competent practitioners who tend to work as a team and attempt to provide preventive and comprehensive care in an atmosphere of suboptimal morale. Many time-honored physician tasks have been delegated to other personnel but the circumstances of reimbursement have eroded a more extensive utilization of pediatric nurse practitioners. There is a system of in-service training and some professional/education relationship does exist with the backup hospital, but is not extensive. Baseline ratings for maintenance care of infants continued to be above the neighborhood health center average and ratings for care of more seriously ill children were outstanding.

IV. Obstetrical-Gynecological Services

A. Obstetrical Baseline Care

Number of records, supplied by center
    personnel, of patients who have delivered at
    least 8 weeks prior to review   23
Number by trimester of registration
    First   9
    Second   11
    Third   3

Only about one-third of the women were registered in their first trimester, not much of an improvement over earlier years. Eight of the 15 under general care at the center prior to their pregnancy came for their initial prenatal workup in the first trimester. Only two of the remainder were registered in the third trimester, including one with a history of a single kidney who delivered four days after her initial visit in the eighth month.

Initial Workup; number with:
    System review   23
    Past obstetrical history   15 (15 ind)
    Family history   23
    Complete urinalysis   21
    Hemoglobin/hematocrit   23
    Serology   23
    Rh and typing   23
    Chest film/tb test   7/15
    Pap smear   21
    Sickle cell preparation   12 (23 ind)
    Vaginal smear   20

In the main, initial workups were complete. The single area of omissions was screening for sickle cell disease in an area predominantly black and Puerto Rican. Some results of studies were omitted from the prenatal flow sheet or were just checked as done—the latter was of little use if specific results were not included. A positive tuberculin test was followed up with a chest x-ray. Antibody titres were obtained on women who were Rh negative, followed later by Rho-GAM immunization when appropriate.

Collaborative Services; number with:
Nutritional counseling	14
Social service visits	—
Dental visits	0
Home visits	9

The prenatal form contained a section for checking off counseling activities or referrals to collaborative services. A fair number of women were afforded diet teaching by the nurse practitioners but beyond the checked-off fact, there was little documentation of the content of the instruction.

Dental records are kept separately but there was no indication that women were receiving dental care.

There were a few home visits, the majority made by staff at the Bathgate clinic. Most visits were made after delivery to check mothers and infants, or to follow up broken appointments.

Prenatal Visits:	ACOG Rec.*	NHC Average	
2nd trimester	3	2.2	3.6
7th month	1	1.4	1.6
8th month	2	1.8	1.7
9th month	4	2.3	3.0

*ACOG: American College of Obstetrics & Gynecology.

Overall, the frequency of prenatal visits was somewhat below the ACOG recommendations in the eighth and ninth months. This seemed to be more of a deficit at the Third Avenue Center than at Bathgate.

Repeat hemoglobin   12 (20 ind)
Repeat serology   7 (20 ind)

Third trimester laboratory studies of serological tests for syphilis and hemoglobin levels were rather inconsistently provided. Considering the generally complete initial laboratory workup, there may be some need to review the procedures with regard to third trimester testing.

Omissions on Prenatal Visits; number of omissions
    on number of patients:
Weight   2 on 2 pts.
Blood pressure   3 on 3 pts.
Urine   20 on 11 pts.

There were occasional lapses with regard to recording weight and blood pressure results at prenatal visits. Documentation of dipstick urinalysis results was more frequently lacking.

Delivery Records; number with recordings for:
Place of delivery   17
Type of delivery   17
Weight of infant   7
Apgar/condition   6

Only five of the 23 records contained complete delivery records from the hospital. Twelve of the remainder contained partial information pertaining to place and type of delivery in progress notes. Only a few of these mentioned the weights and conditions of the infants. Among the remaining 6 women's charts with no delivery information, data were available in three of the infant charts.

Number with:
Postpartum visit   21

Blood pressure	17
Pelvic examination	17
Contraceptive advice	18
Sterilization	4
Infants seen	16

Only two individuals failed to return for postpartum care, and only one failed to obtain contraceptive advice. At the postpartum clinic visits, a few failed to receive the minimum routines of blood pressure and pelvic examination. These included an individual whose blood pressure during the pregnancy ranged from 120-145/70-90 and who had a history of high blood pressure in her previous pregnancy. Another women was found to have an elevated reading of 130/100 at her visit but this was not repeated or followed up.

B. Clinical Management

A review was made of nine obstetrical and ten gynecological charts. The overall review of obstetrical/gynecological care is acceptable both in the ambulatory setting and in the hospital. However, there is room for improvement.

a. Many times laboratory data were properly obtained but the results were not recorded on the prenatal sheets.

b. Often the progress notes on the prenatal sheets were illegible (most commonly by the physician) and incomplete.

c. Routine laboratory work that was supposed to be repeated in the third trimester was apparently not obtained.

d. Hospital reports were often absent in obstetrical patients.

e. Dental referrals are made for routine care only on Medicaid patients (and not all of those) and on others only if they have obvious problems.

f. That part of the prenatal record indicating prenatal teaching by the nurse practitioner was too often mostly blank.

g. The organization of the prenatal record, especially the

section dealing with progress notes, does not permit easy presentation or understanding of the patient's course.

h. Sickle cell preparations were often omitted.

i. There was occasionally a system-induced delay in getting patients into ongoing prenatal care.

j. The lack of apparent concern in one record about an insignificant amount of maternal weight gain over a three-month interval raises questions about whether nutrition is being sufficiently emphasized.

k. The routine use of cervical conization, instead of colposcopically directed biopsy, for evaluation of abnormal Pap smears is questionable.

l. The apparent lack of appreciation of certain categories of obstetrical patients as being exceptionally high-risk is worthy of mention. For example, the current draft of the standard procedures for prenatal patients does not mention amniocentesis for chromosome studies in patients over age 35; decreased growth rate of fetus; underweight mothers; lack of maternal weight gain during pregnancy; etc.

C. Recommendations

1. Ongoing data collection on Martin Luther King obstetrical patients with an annual summary that would include at least:

Number of deliveries
Site of deliveries and provider of care
Number of low birth weight babies
Perinatal mortality rates
Infant mortality rates
Maternal mortality rates
Incidence of cesarean section delivery
Incidence of puerperal morbidity
Number of postpartum tubal ligations

2. Provision of "two minute" pregnancy tests so patients do not have to return for results.

3. Better charting of laboratory data on prenatal records.

4. Revision of prenatal record to improve usefulness and legibility of the progress notes.

5. More emphasis and consideration of fetal well-being during provision of prenatal care.

6. Better attention to obtaining designated repeat routine laboratory studies in third trimester (i.e., STS, GC cultures, Hct).

7. Utilization of colposcopy in evaluation of abnormal Pap smears.

8. Utilization by all teams of a log for patients with a positive serology indicating treatment, follow-up, and investigation of contacts.

9. More vigorous pursuit of contacts of patients with positive gonococcal cultures.

10. Continued pursuit of efforts to improve feedback of information from hospital to Martin Luther King especially for obstetrical patients.

11. More emphasis on nutrition and dental care in prenatal patients and better utilization of dental services by routine referral for those patients not receiving regular dental care.

12. Attempt to interest obstetrical/gynecological department chairman at Bronx-Lebanon in visiting MLK and to get him more involved in an advisory capacity.

13. The addition of certified nurse-midwives would strengthen the program.

14. Efforts should be made to increase the contacts between the team members and the obstetrician/gynecologists.

15. Continued efforts to improve registration for prenatal care in the first trimester should be made.

D. Summary

The concept and the operating system for provision of obstetrical/gynecological care appear to be sound. The relationship between the professional and supporting staff seems to be healthy and productive in the main. The Bronx-Lebanon Hospital relationship appears to be positive and supportive. The patient care and satisfaction seems to be sound and under scrutiny. The number of obstetrician/gynecologists and the patient load seem to be well-balanced. The physician salaries are modest. The nurse practitioner would seem to be very capable and dependable.

Ratings for baseline care continued to remain above the neighborhood health center average. Ratings for clinical management of more seriously ill gynecological patients were satisfactory while ratings for patients with obstetrical complications were slightly below average, primarily due to failure of close follow-up of routines, lack of attention to details of care of some high-risk patients, and poor record-keeping practices.

V. Dental Services

A. Overall Description and Evaluation

The dental department offers comprehensive dental services to the patients of the center. It is staffed by six full-time and five part-time dentists and an adequate supporting staff which includes nine dental assistants, a preventive therapist, two receptionists, two clerks, and a nonprofessional manager of the unit.

Essentially all dental services with the exception of major oral surgery are offered. A full-time pedodontist, and a part-time prosthodontist, periodontist and orthodontist, make this an unusually well-rounded service. The review of records indicates that the patients generally receive services appropriate to their needs.

The quality of dental services, as evidenced from the review of records, seems generally good (see Table 11.3). The diagnostic evaluation is adequate, treatment plans are present in almost all cases (although they are by phases of treatment only), and treatment appears to be appropriate to preexisting conditions.

Deficiencies exist in the quality of radiographic services, as mentioned above, and in some aspects of documentation.

There is a high commitment to quality assessment. Both an internal and external audit procedure is employed, external audits being performed on a rotating basis by the dental

Table 11.3
Central Audit Scores

Center	Date Studied	Overall Score	Major Components				Selected Details			No. of Cases
			Preparation	Treatment	History	X-rays	Treatment Plan	Treatment Progress	Preventive Care	
Average of 73 centers		63	55	68	77	62	26	77	55	
Martin Luther King	4/76	70	63	75	98	54	42	83	83	25

Criterion for case selection was that the patient made at least three visits to the facility over at least a two-month period.

director of some other neighborhood health center in New York and using the vehicle of direct patient examination. The dental staff is to be commended for their work in this area, and areas of deficiency are being addressed in a constructive way.

The dental staff should develop a viable recall system, recognizing that there is a high population turnover in the community. Patients who are brought to a good level of oral health should be maintained there, and some percentage of the patients would certainly respond to expressed interest on the part of the Martin Luther King Jr. Health Center dental staff in helping them to maintain this newly found health level.

The patient record maintained by the dental department is far above average for American dental practices. Involvement in internal audit appears to be a positive force in improving standardization and compliance. However, there are some areas where documentation could be improved, which in turn would provide better data for the audit activity.

The following deficiencies were noted in the patient records:

1. No chief complaint or reason for first encounter.
2. No notation on source of referral.
3. Histories undated and unsigned; no provision for updating histories.
4. In charting, there is no notation of preexisting conditions, only the restorations that are needed; no provision for updating.

5. Data base for patient examination not explicitly defined and is particularly deficient in the area of periodontal status evaluation.
6. No problem list or list of established diagnoses.
7. Treatment plans by categories of services are not particularly useful in planning treatment on a visit-by-visit basis.
8. Progress notes unsigned; having only initials of the provider, which are usually present, makes identification of the provider difficult.
9. Progress note sheet does not carry patient's name or number, and this sheet is loose in the folder.
10. Legibility is a general problem, more so with some providers than others.
11. Some lack of uniformity in terminology and a general lack of uniformity in the content and format of the progress note.
12. Neither internal nor external consultations noted in the record.
13. Relationships to medical record (discharge from dental service, summaries, consult notes, etc.) not noted.

In a center generally committed to use of the problem-oriented format, thought might be given to making the dental record more problem-oriented.

B. Recommendations

1. Greater effort should be made to relate dentistry in a realistic day-to-day basis with the functioning primary care teams. This should include improving the reliability of referrals from primary care to dentistry; working to upgrade oral disease recognition skills of family health workers, pediatricians and internists; and documenting dental care in the medical record.

2. Efforts should be renewed to solve daily operational problems which seem readily amenable to solution. The unit manager system should be reexamined to see if its disadvantages do not outweigh its advantages.

3. The dentists should begin an effort to better define

various parameters of patient care, including the data base for patient examination, format and content of the dental record, and the internal audit procedure. Internal audit should become a more standardized, routine part of the practice. Thought should be given to a problem-oriented approach to the record since there is a commitment to POMR at MLK.

4. Even within the constraints of the payment mechanisms, there should be increased productivity both in numbers of patients seen and in number of services provided per patient visit.

C. Summary

The dental department appeared to have an above average program. Its problems stem in part from its isolation from the remainder of the health service components and from administrative arrangements that are not working optimally.

12
Conclusions
Donald A. Smith, M.D.

The purpose of this book has been to look at how one health center viewed ambulatory quality care assurance. Since other parties (Medicaid, Medicare, and an HEW grant) provide the major funding for the center, we never ourselves felt it our main responsibility to monitor quality as a technique for cost containment. Although overutilization of services does occur in the ambulatory setting, our impression at the Dr. Martin Luther King Jr. Health Center is that omission of important steps in care occurs more often than overutilization. Also, the status of MLK as a non-profit organization with salaried employees who receive no monetary benefit from ordering lab tests removes some incentive for the overutilization of services. Thus, our goal has been to assure our funding sources and ourselves that the quality of services being rendered is of a high standard as determined by current scientific medical principles.

This has been performed through numerous techniques.

1. Assessments of patient satisfaction—questionnaires, patients' rights program.
2. Process reviews—standardization and review of family medical and dental charts, disease review (as for gonorrhea), death review.
3. Outcome reviews—dental, hypertension.

The most difficult question that remains to be asked is whether all the money and effort put into quality care assurance at MLK has truly assured for us the quality of care we hoped for. The term *quality assurance* implies that there are certain predetermined standards of performance toward which one strives. The nearer the goal, the better the quality. As stated before in Chapter 1, the main goal of the health center was to provide health care which was easily accessible, comprehensive, long term, family-oriented, preventive, respectful for the privacy and dignity of those served, and of high quality. Within this context the term "high quality" is partly redundant because the center would argue that high quality should imply most of the other descriptions listed. However, the concept of high quality has additional meanings.

First, it implies rigorous attention to one of the earliest maxims of health care embodied in the Hippocratic Oath, *non nocere*, do no harm. Our death and drug reaction review is specifically geared to this aspect of quality, although all chart review tries to assure this goal of harmlessness.

Second, high quality implies that all procedures for primary prevention—that is, for preventing the occurrence of disease—be applied to each individual. Traditionally, this implies that immunizing procedures for children, pregnant women, and other adults be uniformly performed.

Third, high quality implies that detection of all those diseases for which presymptomatic detection and early therapy may ameliorate the progression of the disease be instituted and repeated periodically. Health maintenance schedules must be devised and applied to all individuals.

Fourth, once disease becomes apparent through screening tests or symptomatic complaints, practitioners must intervene with accurate diagnostic techniques, and appropriate therapeutic and rehabilitive means to lessen morbidity and prolong survival. Hypertensives must be followed carefully to maintain a normo-tensive state. Recurrent asymptomatic bacteriuria in a young woman must be followed closely. The cause of occult blood in the stool must be found and treated appropriately.

The performance of the above tasks with a high degree of quality implies that a health center and its practitioners must take a very assertive role toward the patient population it serves. It means that the center first of all must emphasize health education—the attempt not only to change patient attitudes, but also to promote personal behavior which emphasizes the maintenance of health. Just as diabetics have always been instructed on the detailed daily management of their disease, so must patients with hypertension be taught the importance of continuous blood pressure control in order that they will be responsible for periodic blood pressure checks and the refilling of blood pressure medications. Women must be taught to check their breasts so that they will actually perform this task routinely and report abnormalities promptly.

If educational efforts don't produce the necessary behavioral changes in the patient, then the health center must be willing to go out and try to convince the patient to return for those services beneficial to their health. For example, efficient systems must be devised to help health teams respond to this function of monitoring patients for compliance with health maintenance procedures proven to increase survival and lower morbidity. Women must be recalled for their Pap smears, hypertensives for their medication refills, no-show alcoholics for another try at detoxification.

Such surveillance functions by health practitioners are relatively new. Within the ambulatory setting such functions have become as important in time and effort as are the responses to the complaints of the symptomatic patient. This surveillance of asymptomatic people for presymptomatic disease (early cervical cancer) or asymptomatic disease (hypertension) began after World War II. It has been shown that the natural history of many diseases can be ameliorated by very early intervention. This information has not yet been fully realized or acted upon by the general population. Only a minority of patients within the MLK catchment area come to the center asking for their Pap smears or are primary initiators in the control of their chronic diseases. Therefore, the health center must take the responsibility to initiate action in these monitoring areas of presymptomatic or asymptomatic disease.

Often the responsibility for poor care in follow-up of

disease is placed solely on the patient—"Well, if they don't show up for their appointments, it's their own fault." Literature focuses on patient compliance and the monitoring of patient behavior. Obviously this is important, but if it takes the focus off the practitioner end of the interaction, then the point of intervention to change the system most easily will be missed.

As demonstrated in the chapters on gonorrhea and hypertension, monitoring of practitioner behavior can change behavior toward those parameters which are measured. But the monitoring must be continuous, or practitioner behavior reverts to premeasurement conditions. This is the problem of such outside evaluative activities as described in Chapter 10. A one-time look at a health center can point out deficiencies, but will not necessarily promote changes to improve them. Constant feedback and monitoring are necessary to achieve such changes.

Most practitioners support the concept of monitoring patients with presymptomatic and asymptomatic disease. The tendency to place the blame for noncompliance on the patient stems from the enormous effort required and frustration encountered when practitioners perform these tasks. The thrill of alleviating a bothersome symptom usually has much more immediate personal reward for a practitioner than reassuring an individual that he is healthy on a health maintenance exam or maintaining a normal blood pressure in an asymptomatic patient who has hypertension. "Why get upset if the patient doesn't show for a screening exam but is in general a healthy patient?" How can one practitioner keep up with all the patients on isoniazid prophylaxis, all the hypertensives, all the people needing repeat medical and dental screening exams, all the kids needing immunization shots? The job is overwhelming and can only be performed by looking at one's patients as a population to be monitored rather than looking at each individual. One must not only be able to assure oneself that hypertensives coming in for a checkup have their blood pressure controlled, but also that all hypertensives are, in fact, coming in for checkups.

For this purpose, the individual record system is archaic

because it keeps the focus on one individual. Data systems, either manual or computerized, must be devised to inform teams of practitioners when patients are overdue for certain checkups. Such systems as the Hypertension Surveillance System described in Chapter 9 easily perform this role. In addition, they provide information to a practitioner about how well he's doing with his entire population of patients with similar diseases. His criteria of self-evaluation can go beyond each individual to a whole population of individuals. This allows comparison with others and hopefully provides incentive for improvement in himself, his team, and his whole health center. Future funding for health centers must allow for devising such surveillance systems, which combine both managerial and evaluative functions.

Even without the above systems, some things may be done to give the practitioner an efficient overview of a patient beyond the single page of chart staring him in the face at the time of his visit. Flow sheets for chronic diseases (p. 166) can be efficient ways of getting an overview of a patient's response to therapeutic interventions for his disease and an efficient reminder of when the last lab data was obtained. They, also, may be shown to the patient as a means of educating him about his own disease. A health maintenance check list (p. 208) is essential to remembering when the last health maintenance test or immunization was performed and when the next is required. Important items of patient education placed on a standard physical exam check list may encourage the prospective educator to educate. For example, under the check list for "Breasts—normal □, abnormal □" might be placed the item "Breast self exam taught—yes □, no □" (p. 213).

The main impetus for performing these tasks and creating the necessary systems for implementation will only come when each health center seriously assumes the responsibility for educating their populations to more healthy habits and for monitoring intervention in those diseases which through early and/or continued intervention might improve health or survival.

This book has primarily dealt with the assurance of high quality health services to patients registered for care at the health center. If one takes seriously the idea that the purpose of health care is to promote health, then the function of the health center must expand beyond individual health services into the areas of public health and preventive medicine on the community level. To see homicide and alcoholism as leading causes of death, to witness the constant fear and anxiety with accompanying physical manifestations that plague patients because of the instability and violence of their environment, to continue to see unwanted pregnancies and abortions—all these mock our traditional scope of health care services. Somehow we must come to accept some responsibility to and for the community, at least to the point of educating community members wherever possible on health problems, so that the community itself may organize and initiate environmental changes to promote health.

As a community resource, the health center must expand the concept of primary prevention beyond that of immunization against infectious disease to that of amelioration or elimination of environmental problems that cause disease. This task is especially difficult. The health center must be constantly sensitive to environmental causes of disease through data collected from individual patients. It must effectively communicate this data to community residents. And it must nurture the motivation within the community to try and change these toxic environmental stimuli. Working in such a manner with the community is the macroscopic problem of trying to educate and motivate the unmoving individual patient. But to monitor health centers for these activities as well as for traditional personal health care services may be a stimulus to some thought and action in that direction. To neglect this community area of activity while praising oneself for the high quality of personal health care services delivered would be like praising the man with pie all over his face for the cleanliness of the tip of his nose.

In conclusion then, we have presented the scope of quality care assurance efforts at the Dr. Martin Luther King Jr. Health Center. In some instances we have proven that such efforts have had some salutary effects on health care services provided at MLK. Whether the provision of better health services has significantly improved survival and health in our total population of patients or community remains for future exploration.

When compared with other health centers our health services are above average. When compared with our own goals, we are appalled by the distance we still must travel to attain our own concept of quality. Perhaps we have reached the point where we understand the limitations of our current quality assurance methods in improving practitioner and team performance.

The next step requires the development of managerial methods that will encourage teams to broaden their view from the individual patient to the population of registered patients and even to the community they serve, that will give them a tool for better managing health maintenance and chronic disease, and that will simultaneously and constantly give them feedback on the success of their efforts so that changes they make in the services rendered will be maintained.

Appendix A

The Problem-Oriented Medical Record Manual*

The problem-oriented medical record (POMR) is the method used at the Dr. Martin Luther King Jr. Health Center to record information in the medical chart. All team members—family health workers, nurse practitioners, and physicians, plus all specialty physicians—should use the POMR format to describe what was said and done in a patient encounter on the unit, in the screening clinic, or at home.

This manual describes the use and format of the problem-oriented medical record. If used correctly and consistently, the POMR can increase ease and effectiveness of communication between team members, allowing us to provide higher quality comprehensive care to our patients.

The manual describes the three major aspects of the chart: the data base, the problem list, and progress notes written in SOAP format.

I. The Data Base

The Data Base is the minimum acceptable history, physical examination, and laboratory tests obtained on new patients coming to MLK. It includes information obtained by family health workers on the family structure and housing. Initial information about the whole family goes in the front of the family folder.

*Prepared by: John Allcott and a cast of thousands including especially Joan Silverstein and the Training Department, Drs. Tom Plaut, Charlene Graves, Richard Bernstein, and Jeff Gordon.

Data base forms are available for children, adults, and prenatal patients (see Appendixes C, D, and E).

II. The Problem List

On new patients, as the data base is obtained, the information is analyzed, and problems are defined. A list of the problems can then be made and entered on the problem list. A problem can be listed at any visit even though it may not be clearly defined.

On patients who come to MLK over the course of time, new problems will arise and when they do, they are added to the problem list (see page 155).

All chronic problems are given a title and a number and are transcribed onto the chronic problem list. Temporary problems, however, are given a title and a letter (A, B, C, D) and written in on the Acute/Self-Limited (Temporary) Problem list.

Each problem on the problem list is entered with a date in the "Date" column. This date on the problem list is the date that the problem was first described in a progress note in the chart. In this way, the original description of the problem can be found.

Because each problem is titled, the problem list serves as a table of contents for the chart and because each problem is dated, the problem list serves as an index for the chart.

A. Who Can Enter Problems on the Problem List?

Any member of the team—family health worker, nurse practitioner, physicians, consultants, and screening clinic physicians—may enter a problem on the problem list.

B. What is a Problem?

A problem is something the patient and his or her team agree has a significance for the patient's health and should not be forgotten in the future.

A problem can be *medical*:

a. a diagnosis; e.g., cystic fibrosis, diabetes mellitus.

Figure A.1

THE DR. MARTIN LUTHER KING, JR., HEALTH CENTER

PROBLEM LIST

No.	ACTIVE/CHRONIC PROBLEMS	DATE	INACTIVE/RESOLVED	DATE
1	Health Maintenance	8/10/72		
2	Family Planning, IUD	8/10/72		
3	(Hypertension) Hypertensive Heart Disease	(8/10/72) →	10/10/72	
4	Asthma	8/10/72		
5	Penicillin Allergy	8/10/72		
6	Family Problem, Alcoholic Husband	8/29/72		
7	(Tine Test)-Old Pulmonary TB	(8/29/72) →	9/10/72	
8	G.I. Bleeding	3/13/73	Gastrectomy for ulcer 1952	9/1/72
9	(Cardiomegaly) -- see #3	(9/1/72)		
10	Recurrent Tonsillitis/Adenitis	(3/1/73) →	Tonsillectomy	4/7/73
3A	CHF	11/6/72		
4A	Steroid Rx for asthma	11/6/72		

ACUTE/SELF-LIMITED (TEMPORARY) PROBLEM LIST

No.	PROBLEM TITLE		DATES OF OCCURENCE			
A.	Otitis Media	(8/17/72)				
B.	Tonsillitis -- see #10	(9/1/72)	(1/6/73)	(1/25/73)	(2/14/73)	(2/27/73)
C.	Constipation	(10/5/72)				

b. a physical finding; e.g., congestive heart failure.

c. a symptom; e.g., shortness of breath, backache.

d. abnormal lab findings; e.g., positive sickle test.

e. a therapeutic or prophylactic treatment schedule; e.g., anticoagulants or steroids, family planning methods, or INH prophylaxis.

f. a potential medical problem where the patient is at high risk for the development of disease; e.g., parent with diabetes, mother with breast cancer, penicillin allergy, cigarette smoking.

g. significant past surgery; e.g., status post hysterectomy.

A problem can be *social*; e.g., drug or alcohol abuse, or school problem.

A problem can be *environmental*; e.g., lead paint on walls.

A problem can be *psychological*; e.g., anxiety, delusions.

A problem can be a *family problem*; e.g., mother with TB, alcoholic father.

On MLK's new problem list (see example on page 155) each of the above medical, social, environmental, psychological, or family problems is classified by whether it is an active/chronic problem, an inactive/resolved problem, or an acute/self-limited problem.

Active/Chronic Problems. An active problem is one that is now an active concern of the person and the team. For example; health maintenance, family planning, hypertension, asthma, penicillin allergy, alcoholic husband, or a positive tine test.

Inactive or Resolved Problems. An inactive problem is one that is not presently an active concern of the patient and team, but will need to be remembered because it may have significance in the future. For example, hepatitis, pneumonia, or other problems that started out on the active/chronic problem list but have now completely subsided.

Acute, Self-Limited, or Temporary Problems. Acute, self-limited, or temporary problems are usually episodic illnesses such as otitis media, urinary tract infections, or vaginal discharge. Temporary problems might also include constipation, minor injuries, and accidents. Most screening clinic visits will be for acute, self-limited, or temporary problems. Screening practitioners should enter problems on the appropriate list in accordance with these guidelines.

C. Special Problems

Health Maintenance. On every problem list there should be "Health Maintenance" (HM). Health Maintenance refers to the initial data base and the periodic repeat examinations and preventive procedures (immunizations, Pap smears, etc.). The date on the problem list for Health Maintenance is the date of collection of the initial data base. The health maintenance schedule for children and adults is placed directly under the problem list and is kept up-to-date by the practitioner. Progress notes on health maintenance procedures are written in the problem-oriented format and titled "Health Maintenance."

Family Planning. MLK is particularly interested in family planning (F.P.). Accordingly women 14 years old through menopause should be counseled on family planning and the method indicated on the problem list. For example: F.P.—none, F.P.—IUD.

Family Problems. A family problem is (1) a problem that affects two or more family members, (2) puts a stress on the whole family, or (3) puts other family members at risk for developing that disease or a stress-related condition.

The title of a family problem should describe the condition that puts everyone at risk or under stress. The title of the problem should also note the family number of the person where the initial description of the problem can be found (e.g., see 01, see 02, see 03, etc.). The date entered on the problem list is the date of the initial description in the progress note.

Once a family problem is identified, the title, with the information described in the above paragraph, is written in on the next open line on each family member's problem list. The team member identifying a family problem is responsible for writing in this title on all family members' charts.

Family problems may be medical, psychological, social, or environmental.

Some examples. The problem list of 02 who has an alcoholic husband and a positive tine test herself:

| 6 | Alcoholic 01, see 02 | 8/29/72 | | |
| 7 | Positive Tine Test | 8/29/72 | | |

The chart of an 03 would be as follows:

4	Alcoholic 01, see 02	8/29/72		
5	Positive Tine 02, see 02	8/29/72		

D. Revising the Problem List

It is important to revise the problem list so that the current health status of the patient can be found by glancing at the problem list. Below are several examples of revision:

Inactive/Resolved Problems Activated. Sometimes an Inactive/Resolved problem will become active. When this happens the old title and date are left in place and the new active component is listed in the Active/Chronic list with a new date.

8	G. I. Bleeding ←	3/13/73	Gastrectomy for ulcer 1952	8/10/71

Increased Resolution. When a problem title is more clearly defined, the old title should be circled and an arrow drawn to the new title which is written in.

7	+ Tine Test → Old Pulmonary TB	8/29/72 → 9/10/72		

Consolidating Problems. Some interrelated problems may be consolidated using the number of the problem coming first on the problem list. The second number is not used again.

3	Hypertension Hypertensive Heart			
	Disease	8/10/72 → 10/10/72		
9	Cardiomegaly → see #3	9/1/72		

Frequently Occurring Acute/Self-Limited Problems. Sometimes, generally more than five times a year, an Acute/Self-Limited problem occurs with such great frequency that it needs to be a continuing active concern to the practitioner. When this happens the problem is written in on the Active/

Chronic problem list and the date is written in. Then as each episode is resolved, the date is circled, and new dates are written in for new occurrences. (See tonsillitis example on the problem list, page 155).

New Components of an Old Problem. If one aspect of the disorder becomes prominent or if a new problem arises from an existing one, it is dated and listed as a separate component of that problem. For example:

3	Hypertensive Heart Disease	10/10/72		
	A. Congestive Heart Failure	11/6/72		

Active/Chronic Problems Resolved. An active/chronic problem may become inactive or may be resolved. When this happens the title and date are circled with an arrow to the Inactive/Resolved list and the date is written in. Sometimes a new title will be needed. For example:

10	Recurrent Tonsillitis/Adenitis	3/1/73	Tonsillectomy	4/73

E. Updating the Problem List

In general, if a problem list becomes messy or long and cumbersome, there can be a better statement of what the problems are and consolidations can be made. When this happens, the practitioner should write a brief summary progress note outlining the data for each of the problems and should then write a new problem list with new titles and this new date. The summary should contain all the pertinent information up to that date so that the chart prior to this note will not have to be read to find out what has occurred.

Practitioners may find it useful to write update notes using the data base forms and redo the problem list at the time of the periodic repeat health-maintenance history and physical examinations as outlined in the health maintenance guidelines for adults and for children. In this way, it would be possible to divide thick charts, discarding out of date information, yet retaining the pertinent and current information on the patient's problem. Temporary problems from the old problem list should be brought forward when the repeat health maintenance history and physical and the new problem list is done.

III. Progress Notes

A. SOAP Format

Progress notes should be written in the SOAP format as outlined below:

Number and Title: Each problem having a progress note written on it at a patient encounter is headed with its number (or letter if it is an acute self-limited problem) and title.

Subjective (S): What the patient says. The patient's qualitative and quantitative description of his symptoms relevant to that problem and its treatment. If there is a protocol for a particular problem, then certain set questions must be asked. For example, adult diabetics must be asked questions relating to hyper- and hypoglycemia, and infections.

Objective (O): What is observed about the patient. Objective data include physical exam findings, x-ray and lab results relevant to that problem. If there is a flow sheet for that problem the practitioner may write "see flow sheet" and record the data there. On problems with a protocol, there may be certain set information which must be recorded. For example, adult diabetics must have urine sugar and acetone performed and recorded.

Assessment (A): This portion of the progress note should deal with the analysis of the subjective and objective data. This conclusion should deal with etiology of the problem if not yet determined, adequacy of response to treatment and prognosis. If the subjective and objective seem to match up, then the assessment should be clear; if they don't match up logically, then further investigation is necessary. Making an assessment helps you and others follow the orderly, stepwise thought process to evaluate the patient. In obvious situations, the assessment may be very brief—one or two words. With a complicated patient, you may wish to write a whole paragraph.

Plans (P): Five general areas should be considered in writing the plan for any problem:

1. *Plans for Data Collection (Dx).* Diagnostic tests to determine etiology and to aid management. This is the place for "rule outs" and for the tests ordered to rule out or follow a problem. For example—Dx: 1) R/O iron deficiency anemia with stools for blood X3, serum iron and total iron binding capacity. Hematocrit and retic count in 2 weeks.
2. *Plans for Therapy (Rx).* The treatment plans should be explicit. Prescriptions given should be noted, name and amount of drug, number dispensed, instruction for use, number of refills. For example—Rx $FeSO_4$ 300 mg, #90, ī t.i.d., X2.
3. *Patient Education (Ed).* What was told to the patient about the nature of his problem, its course, and its prognosis should be included. For example—Ed: discussed urine testing; will do foot care next visit.
4. *Referral.* If a referral is made, there ought to be a notation that referral has been initiated, along with the specific questions asked of the specialist, e.g., Referred to ENT for opinion on tonsillectomy.
5. *Return Visits.* Future appointment plans should be clear. For example—return prn; family health worker to reschedule; return 4 weeks.

Below are two examples of progress notes:

Problem #3: Hypertensive Heart Disease

S. Some shortness of breath in past 2 weeks; taking the pills sporadically; no chest pains or ankle swell-

ing, non-productive cough for 3 days.
O. Bp. 170/106, P-90
   Chest: rales, right base; Cor: no S_3
   Ankles: 1+ edema
   Wt., up 4 lbs.
A. Symptomatic from CHF, not taking pills.
P. Dx: R/O pneumonia with stat chest x-ray
   Rx: Hydrodiuril 50 mg., #30, 1 daily, X2
   Ed: Emphasized taking pills daily, return in 2
   weeks, will call her if pneumonia on chest x-ray.

Problem #10: Recurrent Tonsillitis, Strep

S. pain less, appetite better, taking ampicillin
O. Temp. 98; pharynx: tonsils still kissing, but no
   exudate; both T.M.'s scarred.
A. Resolving 5th episode of strep tonsillitis with ade-
   nitis this year alone. This now is a chronic recur-
   ring problem.
P. Dx: change title from acute problem list to chronic
   active list
   Rx: continue Ampicillin 250 mg. q.i.d.
   Referral: to ENT: opinion on tonsillectomy?
   Return: in 2 weeks after ENT consult.

B. Special Progress Notes

Home Visits. Family health worker, nurse practitioners,
and physicians should record their home visits in the same
format as patient encounters in the health center. Accordingly, each note should be headed with a number (or letter if
the problem is acute self-limited) and title of the problem
and, in addition, have as part of the title "Home Visit." The
note itself should be written in the SOAP format.

If a home visit is made on a problem for which there is
not a title, the note is given the title "Home Visit," together
with the purpose of the visit. For example, "Home Visit,
follow-up of no-show."

If a home visit turns up a new problem not on the problem list, the team member should give the problem a title and
enter it on the problem list as outlined before.

Below are examples of home visit notes made on August 29, 1972.

#3 Hypertension—Follow-up of No-Show

S. Couldn't make the appointment with Dr. Smith because of problems with husband and kids; not taking pills.
O. BP sitting, 170/106
A. BP not controlled and she isn't taking the pills. See also new problem #6.
P. Rx: Hydrodiuril 50 mg., one each day; to see Dr. Smith in 2 weeks.

#6 Family Problem—Alcoholic Husband

S. Husband is drinking again and has been off and on for past 5 years. She isn't working so that she can take care of him. Many arguments about money. Children having problems at school.
O. Husband not at home; walks slow; difficulty getting up.
A. Family problem with alcohol; she is tired and worn out.
P. Discuss situation with Dr. Smith and talk with her again before next appointment. Will put this problem on all family members' problem lists.

Social Problems. Family health workers should describe the problem as specifically as they can, i.e., "poor housing" or "needs homemaker services" states the problem better than "social problem." Also complex family and social problems are often interrelated (for example, alcoholism, marital problems, unemployment) and these should either be subdivisions of the general problem or listed separately, so that the progress or change in each aspect can be described. It should be remembered that all family problems should be entered on each family member's problem list.

Telephone Calls. Family health workers receive telephone calls from patients on many different matters, including appointments, agency contacts, transportation, and medication. Obviously, they will have to use their own judgment concerning the importance of the information transmitted via the phone call and whether it should be recorded in the chart, since recording of all phone calls from patients would be impossible.

Telephone calls relating to known patient problems could be recorded like this:

Date (#2) Telephone Call—Hypertension

S. What patient tells you (summarized)
O. May have nothing here except description of tone of voice; e.g., patient very upset
A. Status of problem (needs medication refill)
P. What you are going to do about the problem

If someone other than the patient calls you, this should be clearly stated in the progress note.

Accompanying patients to specialty clinics and similar outside agency contacts. These trips can be generally recorded in the category of Patient Assistance. Again the progress note should be brief. Any information that you learned that is important for the patient's future health should be stated. An example might be:

Date (#3) Urination (Pt. Assistance)

S. None
O. Accompanied patient to G-U Clinic at Montefiore. Dr. Cheeky there said patient has enlarged prostate; will need monthly prostatic massage.
A. Clinic visit completed
P. Appt. G-U Clinic 6 months

Notify Dr. S. of above

Counselling. At times, family health workers (as well as other team members) will be providing counselling services to patients. This might include explaining how to cope with a child's behavior or helping family members to adjust to a patient's mental illness.

Again your advice (that is, patient education) to the family as well as your observations of the situation should be recorded in a summarized fashion.

Confidential Information. Family health workers may often be the first members of the team to become aware of problems of a confidential nature. When a patient informs you that what he or she tells you is to be confidential, you have an obligation to make certain it remains so. In these cases, it is best initially to be as general and vague as you can in stating the nature of the problem (label as personal problem, family conflict, marital problem, or emotional problem). Do not state any details on the chart, but note that you can be contacted for further information.

It is also true that it is important for the patient's care that this problem be recorded on the chart. A way to facilitate this is to inform the patient that you will need to make a note on the chart but tell her/him exactly what you are going to write there and that the chart will state this is confidential information. As an example:

Date (#7) Marital Problem (new problem)

S. Mrs. J. told me about recent marital problem
O. Mrs. J. was upset during our talk
A. Marital problem, confidential
P. Refer to Dr. A., appt. in 1 week; discuss with Dr. A. in private; encourage patient to express problems to doctor.
    Reassured her information to remain confidential.

C. Flow Sheets

For certain interrelated problems, progress notes are not an adequate means of relating the multiple variables for following the problems. Construction of a good flow sheet enables the practitioner to assemble a lot of important data at a glance. Flow sheets should be tailor-made to fit the problem or problems and kept up to date by the practitioner. Chronic problems such as asthma with prednisone treatment, diabetes, and hypertension are diseases that are particularly suited for flow sheets. The following is a sample of a flow sheet. The practitioner should indicate parameters to be recorded by writing them in. (See Figure A.2.)

Figure A.2

				THE DR. MARTIN LUTHER KING JR. HEALTH CENTER LABORATORY SUMMARY SHEET	NAME_____ PE #_____			

Date of Test	Weight	B.P. (R)	MEDICATIONS				BUN/K+	HCT.
1/10/73	215	180/115	HCTZ 50qd	Aldomet 250tid			16/4.3	
1/14/73	217	190/117	50bid		KCL-pkt qd			
2/15/73	216	150/95	pt. stopped med	250tid				32
3/13/73	220	145/70				FeSO4 300tid		
4/22/73	221	148/92		skin rash				36
				Apres 25qid				
5/22/73	218	150/90						

<u>USE OF ARROWS</u>

Indicate that the drug was given on this day and was intended to be taken until the next visit.

Indicates that drugs were taken up until the present visit.

Absence of the arrow indicates that the patient stopped meds. and is not taking them.

Appendix B

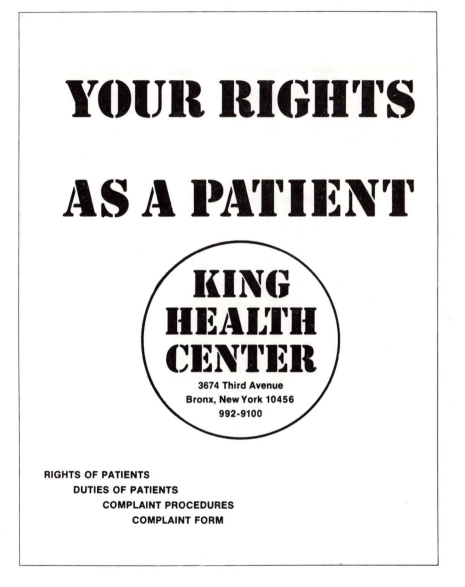

YOUR RIGHTS

AS A PATIENT

KING HEALTH CENTER

3674 Third Avenue
Bronx, New York 10456
992-9100

RIGHTS OF PATIENTS
DUTIES OF PATIENTS
COMPLAINT PROCEDURES
COMPLAINT FORM

TO THE PATIENT

    This booklet was prepared to remind you that you have rights as a patient. Health Center staff have a duty to respect these rights. But if this does not happen, you should insist that your rights be respected. Your duties as a patient are also mentioned.

    If you believe your rights have not been respected, speak to the employee involved at once. If you are not satisfied with the results of this, call Liery Wynn of the Community Health Advocacy Department (ext. 391) or fill out the attached complaint form and send it to him.

    The Health Center has said that it takes this handbook and the rights spelled out in it very seriously. We hope that it will help insure dignity and mutual respect in Health Center and patient relationships.

    This patients' rights booklet was written mainly for patients and staff at the Dr. Martin Luther King Health Center in the Bronx. It is our hope that patients and staff elsewhere will use this as a basis for similar efforts in their own institutions.

———————————————

Liery Wynn, Community Health Advocacy Department
400 East 169 Street, Bronx, New York   10456
992-9100 - ext. 391

PATIENT'S RIGHTS

DIGNITY

You have the right to be treated with respect. You should be called Mr. Jones, not number 231, and not Jones.

RIGHTS IN THE TREATMENT ROOM

a) The patient has a right to consent to, or refuse any treatment.

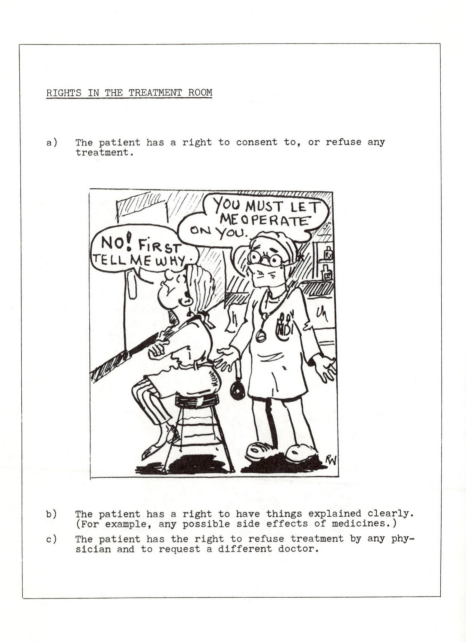

b) The patient has a right to have things explained clearly. (For example, any possible side effects of medicines.)

c) The patient has the right to refuse treatment by any physician and to request a different doctor.

PRIVACY

a) No employee should talk to you about your problems in the waiting room or halls or where others may hear.

b) No one should call across the room for personal information. For example, "Do you have Medicaid?" etc.

c) You have a right to consent to any visit to your home.
    If at all possible you should know in advance when the
    visit will take place.

d) You have a right to refuse to participate in or be inter-
    viewed for research purposes. You have the right to full
    explanation of purposes and uses of the information if you
    do participate.

APPOINTMENT RIGHTS

a) You have a right to choose a convenient time for your
    appointment, if it is available. You should be told what
    times are available.

b) The patient has a right to be notified, in advance when-
    ever possible, when his regular doctor cannot keep an
    appointment. He does not have to see a substitute un-
    less he wants to. The patient may refuse to see a sub-
    stitute and ask to be rescheduled with his regular doctor.

CONFIDENTIALITY

    a)   The patient has a right to have all information about him held in strict confidence by Health Center staff.

    b)   The patient has a right to see letters, know about conferences about him and results of conferences. (Patients must sign all letters.)

OTHER RIGHTS

a) The patient should be told a telephone number where he
    can call his doctor, public health nurse, and family
    health worker.

b) If you are incapacitated, you are entitled to transpor-
    tation to and from the Health Center. Ask your family
    health worker or public health nurse to arrange for this
    service.

c) You can receive help in applying for Medicaid. Contact
    the Front Reception Desk for this service.

d) The patient has a right to request the Health Center
    staff to meet with school personnel about school problems.
    Contact your family health worker concerning this
    service.

e) Patients have certain rights in relation to mental
    institution commitment and child welfare referrals.
    For more information about this contact Mr. Wynn (ext. 391)

f) You have a right to know what's going on. Always ask
    questions about anything that you do not understand or
    that is worrying you.

PATIENT'S DUTIES

a) Patients should keep appointments. If you cannot keep
    an appointment, call your unit receptionist as early
    as possible so that another patient may be scheduled
    in your place.

b) The patient should bring with him to the Health Center
    the name and address of other physicians that he has
    been seeing, or the clinic cards of any clinic he has
    attended. This will enable the Health Center staff to
    send for old records that may help give you better
    health care.

c) You should be frank about the medical instructions of
    the Center staff. If for any reason you feel you can-
    not or should not follow recommendations, talk to the
    staff member right away.

MARTIN LUTHER KING JR. HEALTH CENTER
3674 Third Avenue
Bronx, New York 10456

COMPLAINT PROCEDURE

Liery Wynn of the Community Health Advocacy Department will serve as the patient's advocate for complaints related to the patient's right booklet within the following complaint procedure. The staff member complained about may choose anyone, inside or outside the agency, to serve as his advocate.

When a patient reports a complaint, Mr. Wynn will:

STAGE I

    A. Write it out on a complaint form.

    B. Give a copy to the patient and a copy to any staff member(s) involved in the incident.

    C. Meet with the staff person involved and the patient if he wishes to be present.

STAGE II

    If the patient is not satisfied, Mr. Wynn will take the complaint to the supervisor. Within five (5) days the supervisor will report any action he has taken to correct the situation. Mr. Wynn will report this back to the patient.

STAGE III

    If the patient is still not satisfied, Mr. Wynn will set up a conference at which the project director will review the complaint. The project director, after hearing both sides will decide what action should be taken to deal with the complaint and to prevent similar incidents in the future.

    The following people will be invited to be present at the conference:

      The project director
      The patient
      Mr. Wynn, patient's representative
      The staff person involved
      The staff person's representative
      The staff member's department head or supervisor.

STAGE IV

    If several patients have reported similar complaints, Mr. Wynn will recommend changes in the system so that similar problems will not come up again.

MARTIN LUTHER KING JR. HEALTH CENTER
3674 Third Avenue
Bronx, New York 10456

COMPLAINT FORM

    This form is to be used to report any complaint about the way the Health Center functions or about the service given by anyone (doctor, nurse, receptionist, etc.) who works in the center.

    The Martin Luther King Jr., Health Center is here to provide office medical care to part of the Southeast Bronx Community. It is not a clinic. It is a Health Center where many doctors, nurses, and other trained persons work together to give you high quality, complete, family medical care.

PATIENT'S NAME:_____

ADDRESS:_____

TELEPHONE#:_____TEAM_____

COMPLAINT: (where, when, what happened or did not happen)

STAFF PERSON (if any) INVOLVED:_____

DEPARTMENT:_____POSITION:_____

Please return this form to Liery Wynn, Community Health Department, 400 East 169th Street or call him at 992-9100, ext. 391 Mr. Wynn will contact you and take the necessary steps in handling your complaint.

SUS DERECHOS

COMO UN PACIENTE

**KING
CENTRO
DE SALUD**

3674 Tercera Avenida
Bronx, Nueva York 10456
992-9100

DERECHOS DE LOS PACIENTES
DEBERES DE LOS PACIENTES
PROCEDIMIENTOS EN CASOS DE QUEJAS
FORMA PARA REFERIR QUEJAS

PARA EL PACIENTE

Este librete ha sido preparado para hacerle saber que
Ud., como un paciente, tiene sus derechos. El personal del
Centro de Salud tiene el deber de respetar estos derechos.
Pero si esto no sucede, Ud. debe insistir en que sus derechos
sean respetados. Sus deberes como un paciente tambien estan
mencionados.

Si Ud. cree que sus derechos no han sido respetados, hable
con el empleado envuelto en el asunto al instante. Si Ud. no
se encuentra satisfecho con los resultados, llame al Senor L. Wynn
del Departamento Legal del Centro de Salud, extension 391, o
llene la forma adjunta para referir quejas y enviesela a el.

El Centro de Salud sostiene que trata este librete y los
derechos descritos en el mismo, muy seriamente. Nosotros esperamos
que el mismo ayudara a asegurar dignidad y respeto mutuo en
las relaciones entre el Centro de Salud y el paciente.

Este librete sobre los derechos de los pacientes fue escrito
principalmente para pacientes y personal del Centro de Salud,
Dr. Martin Luther King, en el Bronx. Es nuestra esperanza que
pacientes y personal en cualquier otro sitio usen esto como una
base para esfuerzos similares en sus propias instituciones.

Liery Wynn, Departamento Legal, King Centro De Salud
400 Este - Calle 169, Bronx, Neuva York, 10456
992-9100 - ext. 391

DERECHOS DEL PACIENTE

DIGNIDAD

Ud. tiene derecho de ser tratado con respeto.

Ud. debe ser llamado Senor Diaz, no numero 231, o Diaz.

DERECHOS EN LA SALA DE TRATAMIENTO

a) El paciente tiene derecho a aceptar o rechazar cual-
    quier tratamiento.

b) El paciente tiene derecho de que le expliquen las
    cosas claramente. (Por ejemplo, cualquier posible efecto
    secundario o reaccion de las medicinas.)

c) El paciente tiene el derecho a rehusar tratamiento de
    parte de cualquier medico y solicitar otro doctor en
    su lugar.

PRIVACIDAD

a) Ningun empleado debe hablarle a Ud. acerca de sus problemas en la sala de espera o pasillos o donde otros puedan oir.

b) Nadie debe llamar a traves de la sala para pedir informacion personal. Por ejemplo, "Tiene Ud. Medicaid?"

c) Ud. tiene el derecho a no admitir visitas a su hogar
sin su consentimiento. Si es posible, Ud. debe saber
por adelantado acerca de cualquier visita a su hogar
y cuando la visita tomara lugar.

d) Ud. tiene el derecho de negarse a participar o ser
entrevistado para propositos de estudios. Si participa,
Ud. tiene derecho a que se le de una explicacion
detallada sobre los propositos y usos de la informacion.

DERECHOS PARA CITA

a) Ud. tiene derecho a escoger el dia y la hora con-
   veniente para su cita, si ese tiempo lo hay
   disponibles.

b) El paciente tiene derecho a ser notificado por adelantado, siempre que sea posible, cuando su doctor
   regular no pueda cumplir con una cita. El paciente
   no tiene que ver a un medico substituto a menos que
   lo desee. El puede negarse a ver un medico substituto
   y solicitar una nueva cita con su doctor regular.

CONFIDENCIALIDAD

a) El paciente tiene el derecho de que toda informacion relacionada con el sea mantenida <u>en estricta confidencia</u> por el personal del Centro de Salud.

b) El paciente tiene derecho a ver cartas, saber de conferencias relacionadas con el y los resultados de la conferencias. (Los pacientes deben firmar todas las cartas.)

<u>OTROS DERECHOS</u>

a) Al paciente se le debe dar un numero de telefono
donde pueda llamar a su doctor, enfermera de salud
prblica (Public Health Nurse) y trabajdora de salud
de familia (Family Health Worker).

b) Si Ud. esta incapacitado(a), tiene derecho a trans-
portacion al Centro de Salud y del Centro de Salud
de familia o a la enfermera de salud publica para
hacer arreglos para este servicio.

c) Ud. puede recibir ayuda para aplicar para Medicaid.
Pongase en contacto con la recepcionista en el primer
piso para este servicio.

d) El paciente tiene derecho a requerir del personal del
Centro de Salud una entrevista con las autoridades
escolares para tratar sobre problemas relacionados con
la escuela. Comuniquese con su trabajadora de salud
de familia acerca de este servicio.

e) Los pacientes tienen ciertos derechos en relacion a
recluimiento en instituciones mentales y referimentos
para el bienestar de ninos. Para mas informacion
acerca de esto, pongase en contacto con el Sr. Wynn
(992-9100, extension 391)

f) Ud. tiene el derecho de saber lo que sucede en su
caso. Siempre haga preguntas sobre cualquier cosa
que no entienda o que le este preocupando.

DEBERES DE LOS PACIENTES

a) Los pacientes deben asistir a sus citas. Si Ud. no puede estar presente en una cita, llame a la recepcionista de su unidad tan pronto como le sea posible de modo que otro paciente pueda acomodarse en su lugar.

b) El paciente debe traer consigo al Centro de Salud el nombre y direccion de otros medicos que lo hayan visto, o las tarjetas de clinica de cualquier clinica donde haya sido atendido. Esto permitira al personal del Centro de Salud solicitar los registros (records) anteriores que pueden ayudar a darle mejor tratamiento medico.

c) Ud. debe ser franco(a) en cuanto a las instrucciones medicas que reciba del personal del Centro. Si por cualquier razon Ud. cree que no puede o no debe seguir las recomendaciones, hable con el miembro del personal encargado del asunto inmediatamente.

CENTRO DE SALUD
DR. MARTIN LUTHER KING, JR.
3674 Tercera Avenida
Bronx, Nueva York 10456

PROCEDIMIENTOS EN CASOS DE QUEJAS

Liery Wynn del Departamento Legal del Centro de Salud de la Comunidad servira como defensor al paciente en quejas relacionadas con los derechos del paciente segun se describen en el librete "SUS DERECHOS COMO UN PACIENTE"

El(los) miembro(s) del personal del(de los) cual(es) se han quejado puded(n) seleccionar a cualquiera, dentro o fuera de la agencia, para servir como su(s) abogado(s).

CUANDO UN PACIENTE PRESENTE UNA QUEJA, EL SENOR WYNN HARA LO SIGUIENTE:

PASO I

A. Escribiralo referido en una forma de quejas.

B. Dara copia al paciente y una copia al(a los) miembro(s) del personal envuelto(s) en el incidente.

C. Reunira con el(los) empleado(s) envuelto(s) y con el paciente si el desea estar presente.

PASO II

Si el paciente no esta satisfecho, el Sr. Wynn llevara la queja al supervisor. Dentro de cinco (5) dias el supervisor le informara al Sr. Wynn sobre cualquier accion que el haya tomado para corregir la situacion. El Sr. Wynn le dejara saber esto al paciente.

PROCEDIMIENTOS EN CASOS DE QUEJAS   (cont'd)

PASO III

Si el paciente aun no esta satisfecho, el Sr. Wynn
llevara a cabo una conferencia en la cual el director del
proyecto revisara la queja. El director del proyecto,
despues de oir ambas partes, decidira la accion que debe
tomarse para tratar sobre la queja y evitar incidentes
similares en el futuro.

Las siguientes personas seran invitadas para estar
presentes en la conferencia:

> El director del proyecto
>
> El paciente
>
> El Sr. Wynn, representante del paciente
>
> El (los) representante(s) del (de los) empleado(s)
>
> El jefe del departamento o supervisor del (de los)
> empleado(s)

PASO IV

Si varios pacientes han presentado quejas similares,
el Sr. Wynn recomendara cambios en el sistema de tal manera
que los mismos problemas no surjan otra vez.

CENTRO DE SALUD
DR. MARTIN LUTHER KING, JR.
3674 Tercera Avenida
Bronx, Nueva York 10456

FORMA PARA REFERIR QUEJAS

Esta forma es para ser usada para referir cualquier queja sobre la forma como funciona el Centro de Salud o sobre los servicios dados por los empleados (como doctores, enfermeras, recepcionistas, etcetera).

El Centro de Salud, Dr. Martin Luther King, Jr. esta aqui para proveerle cuidado medico a parte de la comunidad del sur-este del Bronx. No es una clinica. Es un Centro de Salud donde muchos doctores, enfermeras y otras personas entrenadas trabajan juntas para darle a Ud. un cuidado medico de familia completo y de alta calidad.

NOMBRE DEL PACIENTE: _____

DIRECCION: _____

TELEFONO #: _____   GRUPO: _____

QUEJA: (donde, cuando, que sucedio o que no sucedio)

_____

_____

_____

_____

_____

_____

_____

_____

MIEMBRO(S) DEL PERSONAL ENVUELTO(S) (SI ALGUNO(S))

_____ , _____ , _____

DEPARTAMENTO: _____   PUESTO(S) QUE OCUPA(N) _____

Favor de devolver esta forma al Sr. Liery Wynn, Departamento de Salud de la Comunidad, 400 Este calle 169 o llamelo al telefono 992-9100, extension 391. El Sr. Wynn se comunicara con Ud. y tomara los pasos necesarios para tratar sobre su queja.

Appendix C

MLK Pediatric Health Supervision Schedule and Forms

MLK Pediatric Health Supervision Schedule

Age	Immunizations	Standard Procedure	Lab	Examiner
1 month	DPT #1-Polio #1 (Trivalent)		Urine	N.P.-Ped.
2 months	DPT #2			N.P.
3 months	DPT #3-Polio #2 (Trivalent)			N.P.
5 months	Trivalent Polio #3			N.P.-Ped.
8 months		Tine	Hct	N.P.
12 months	Live measles Vac.		Hct Urine S-Prep	
18 months	DPT Booster #1 Trivalent Polio #4			N.P.
2 years	*Rubella & Mumps	Tine	Hct Urine	Ped.
3 years		Tine	Hct Urine	N.P.
4 years	**Trivalent oral Polio #5 DPT Booster #2	Tine Vision ***Hearing	Hct Urine	N.P.
5 years		Vision Tine	Hct Urine	Ped.
6 years		Vision Tine	Hct Urine	N.P.
7 years		Vision Tine	Hct Urine	Ped.
8 years		Vision Tine	Hct Urine	N.P.
9 years		Vision Tine	Hct Urine	Ped.
11 years		Vision Tine	Hct Urine	N.P.
13 years		Tine Vision Hearing	Hct Urine	Ped.
15 years	Td Adult 14-16 (Ten years after last booster).	Vision Tine	Hct Urine	N.P.

*   Rubella and Mumps vaccine may be given at anytime after the first birthday. They may be given singly, together or with measles vaccine - provided all three are made by Merck-Sharpe & Dohme.
**   DPT booster and oral polio #5 may be given anytime between the 4th and 6th birthday.
***   Hearing test is attempted at the 4th birthday. If successful it is repeated at age 12-14. If unsuccessful it is repeated until okay or child is referred to speech and hearing.

Figure C.1

TEAM

NAME   PEDIATRIC HEALTH MAINTENANCE SHEET

ADDRESS   (0-15)

B.D.

IMMUNIZATIONS: (record month and year received)

DPT:_____,_____,_____,_____,_____,   Td:_____

OPV:_____,_____,_____,_____,

Measles:_____Mumps:_____Rubella:_____Smallpox:_____,_____

Others:

Health Maintenance Visits:
                              Date   Result

Sickle Prep: ____   ____

Audiometry: ____   ____

                              ____   ____

Denver Developmental   ____   ____
Screening Test:

                              ____   ____

Age	0-6 mos.	7-12 mos.	2	3	4	5	6	
Year								
Exam								
Hct								
UA								
Tine								
R eye								
L eye								

Age	7	8	9	11	13	15		
Year								
Exam								
Hct								
UA								
R eye								
L eye								

Figure C.2

THE DR. MARTIN LUTHER KING, JR. HEALTH CENTER

0 – 5 YEARS
INITIAL AND INTERVAL VISITS

DATE _____ AGE _____

TEMP. _____ P_____ R_____ HT. _____ WT. _____ BP. _____ HC. _____

A. Feeding & Nutrition

B. Habits

C. Development (Socialization)

General Appearance _____

Skin _____ Abdomen _____
Nodes _____ Umbilicus _____
Head (AF) _____ Liver _____
  eyes _____ Hernia _____
  ears _____ Femoral Pulse _____
  nose _____ Other _____
  throat _____ Back & Spine _____
  teeth _____ Genitalia _____
Neck _____   male _____
Thorax _____   female _____
Heart _____ Extremities _____
Lungs _____ Neuro _____
  Muscle tone _____
  Cry _____

CHECK PROBLEM AREA AND ELABORATE BELOW

HISTORY REVIEW

☐ Infections
☐ Hospitalizations
☐ Accidents
☐ Allergies

SYSTEM REVIEW

☐ EENT
☐ Respiratory
☐ Cardio-vascular
☐ GI

☐ GU
☐ Neuro
☐ Bones, Muscles & Joints
☐ Behavior Problems

Problems: (If initial visit, include maternal, perinatal, neonatal)

Impression:

Plan:

RV Plan

Signature _____

FORM NO. MED. 4 REV. 6/71   Continue on Back Page

Figure C.3

THE DR. MARTIN LUTHER KING, JR. HEALTH CENTER

6 – 15 YEARS
INITIAL AND INTERVAL VISITS

DATE _____ AGE _____

TEMP. _____ P _____ R _____ HT. _____ WT. _____ BP. _____

A. School
    Grade _____
    Best Subjects _____
    Academic _____
    Performance _____

B. Nutrition

C. Socialization

D. Habits

General Appearance _____
_____
Skin _____
Nodes _____
EENT _____
Teeth _____
Chest _____
    Heart _____
    Lungs _____
Abdomen _____
Genitalia (Hernia) _____
Back & Spine _____
Extremities _____
Neuro _____
Other _____

CHECK PROBLEM AREA AND ELABORATE BELOW

HISTORY REVIEW

☐ Infections
☐ Hospitalizations
☐ Accidents
☐ Allergies

SYSTEM REVIEW

☐ EENT   ☐ GU
☐ Respiratory   ☐ Neuro
☐ Cardio-vascular   ☐ Bones, Muscles & Joints
☐ GI   ☐ Behavior Problems

Problems: (If initial visit, include maternal, perinatal, neonatal)

Impression:

Plan:

RV Plan

Signature _____

Appendix D

Adult Health Maintenance
Schedule (By Age)

Age 16–39
Initial Visit

Male	Female
History	History
P.E.	P.E. with Pap, GC cultures
Chest x-ray PPD	Chest x-ray PPD
CBC Sickle prep. VDRL Urinalysis	CBC Sickle prep. VDRL Urinalysis (clean catch)
Casual sugar BUN Cholesterol Triglycerides Ova and parasites*	Casual sugar BUN Cholesterol Triglycerides Ova and parasites*
Tetanus diphtheria immunization (if last Td shot over 10 yrs. ago)	Tetanus diphtheria immunization (if last Td shot over 10 yrs. ago) Rubella vaccination (see p. 206)

---

*Ova and parasites check only for:

A. Puerto Ricans who have moved to U.S.A. within past 5 years.
B. Other Puerto Ricans who have visited P.R. more than twice in last 5 years.
C. Blacks who moved from South in last 5 years.
D. Vietnam veterans.

Every 3 Years

History (Complete ROS and
    update all else)

Weight
BP
VDRL
PPD

History (complete ROS and
    update all else)

Weight
BP
VDRL
PPD
Pelvic with Pap, GC cultures
    (after 2 negative consecutive
    annual Paps)
Crit
Urinalysis (clean catch)

Every 10 Years

Tetanus diphtheria immunization   Tetanus diphtheria immunization

Age 40–64
Initial Visit*
(First visit after age 40 of those who have been coming regularly to MLK)

Male

History (complete ROS and
    update other)

P.E. including rectal

Chest x-ray
PPD
EKG

Female

History (complete ROS and
    update other)

P.E. including rectal, Pap, GC
    cultures (to age 50)

Chest x-ray
PPD
EKG

If first visit ever to MLK, do the following in addition to the above:
Sickle prep
WBC and diff. (total CBC instead of crit only)
Triglycerides
Ova and parasites if meets criteria
Tetanus diphtheria immunization (if last Td shot over 10 years ago)

Hematocrit
VDRL
Urinalysis
Stool occult blood X6
  (if 55 and over)

Casual sugar
BUN
Cholesterol
LFT's (SGOT, alk. phos., LDH)

Hematocrit
VDRL
Urinalysis (clean catch)
Stool occult blood X6
  (if 55 and over)

Casual sugar
BUN
Cholesterol
LFT's (SGOT, alk. phos., LDH)

Every 3 Years

History (complete ROS and
  update other)

Weight
BP

History (complete ROS and
  update other)

Weight
BP
Breast exam
Pelvic with Pap, GC cultures (after
  2 negative consecutive annual
  Paps)

PPD

PPD

Hematocrit
VDRL
Urinalysis (if 55 and over)
Stool occult blood X6
  (if 55 and over)

Casual sugar
BUN

Hematocrit
VDRL
Urinalysis (clean catch)
Stool occult blood X6
  (if 55 and over)

Casual sugar
BUN

Every 6 Years

Male

Chest x-ray (non-smoker)
EKG

Female

Chest x-ray (non-smoker)
EKG

Every 10 Years

Tetanus diphtheria immunization   Tetanus diphtheria immunization

Special Tests

Women with (a) fibrocystic mastitis or (b) a family history of breast cancer (grandparents, parents, sibs) should have manual breast exam every year, mammography every 3 years.

Smokers: If greater than or equal to 1 pack per day, check x-ray every 1 year.
If less than or equal to 1 pack per day, chest x-ray every 3 years.

Age 65 and Over
Initial Visit*
(First visit of patient at 65 who has been coming regularly to MLK)

Male	*Female*
History (complete ROS, update other)	History (complete ROS, update other)
P.E. including rectal exam	P.E. including rectal exam and Pap
Chest x-ray	Chest x-ray
PPD	PPD
EKG	EKG
Hematocrit	Hematocrit
VDRL	VDRL
Urinalysis	Urinalysis (clean catch)
Stool occult blood X6	Stool occult blood X6
Casual sugar	Casual sugar
BUN	BUN
LFT's (SGOT, alk. phos., LDH)	LFT's (SGOT, alk. phos., LDH)

If first visit ever to MLK, do the following in addition to the above:
Sickle prep
WBC and diff (total CBC instead of crit only)
Ova and parasites if meets criteria
Tetanus diphtheria immunization (if last Td shot over 10 yrs. ago)

Every Year

Male	*Female*
History (complete ROS, update other)	History (complete ROS, update other)
Weight	Weight
Flu shot	Flu shot

Every 2 Years

Male	*Female*
Stool occult blood X6	Stool occult blood X6

Every 3 Years

History	History
Weight	Weight
BP, HR	BP, HR
Rectal/prostate exam	Breast exam
	Pelvic with rectal, Pap
PPD	PPD
EKG	EKG
Hematocrit	Hematocrit
Urinalysis	Urinalysis (clean catch)

Every 6 Years

Chest x-ray (non-smoker)	Chest x-ray (non-smoker)

Every 10 Years

Tetanus diphtheria immunization	Tetanus diphtheria immunization

Special Tests

Women with (a) fibrocystic mastitis or (b) a family history of breast cancer (grandparents, parents, sibs) should have manual breast exam every year, mammography every 3 years.

Smokers: If greater than or equal to one pack per day, chest x-ray every year. If less than one pack per day, chest x-ray every 3 years.

Rubella Vaccination

In 1969, the U.S. Public Health Service Committee on immunization practices recommended the administration of Rubella Vaccine to all children 1 year of age to puberty. Since then a number of articles have been published on the beneficial and adverse effect of Rubella vaccination. Other articles have appeared on the merits of the experimental RA 27/3 Rubella Vaccine which is given intranasally.

Following is the schedule of Rubella vaccination for MLK intra-agency use. It was approved at the combined internist, pediatric, nurse practitioner meeting on March 2, 1977.

Pediatric Schedule

1. Pre-school boys and girls.

Give Rubella vaccine individually or part of MMR vaccine (at 15 months).

2. Boys and girls already in school with:
   a) Known history of Rubella vaccination administration, or

   a) No Rubella vaccination.

   b) Past history of Rubella infection.

   b) Do HAI titer for Rubella. If negative, give Rubella vaccination.

3. Girls 12 years to puberty.

Do HAI titer for Rubella. If negative give Rubella vaccination.

Adolescent and Young Female Adults

1. All women capable of child bearing with no past history of Rubella vaccination.

Do HAI Rubella titer. If negative, give Rubella vaccine immediately following a menstrual period to those who give informed consent, i.e., those who understand the side effects and who agree to avoid pregnancy for two months. A note to that effect must be written in the chart. If the person is less than 18 years of age, a parent must be aware that the patient will get the vaccine and that pregnancy is contraindicated for two months.

2. All pregnant women with previous positive titer ≥ 1/32, or documented history of receiving Rubella vaccination.

Do not do further titer. Do not immunize.

All other pregnant women.

Do HAI titer. If ≤ 1/8, give Rubella vaccine in immediate postpartum to those who give informed consent as described above.

If ≥ 1/16, do not immunize.

Figure D.1

Sickle Prep_____ WBC_____

Dr. Martin Luther King Jr. Health Center

Adult Health Maintenance

Flow Sheet

	DATE												
HISTORY	PH,FH,HABITS FORM												
	ROS. FORM												
PHYSICAL	General												
	Pelvic												
	PAP Smear												
	GC Culture												
	Visual Acuity												
LAB	▮▮▮ HCT.												
	Urinalysis												
	VDRL												
	SMA 12												
	PPD												
	Triglycerides												
	Stool Hemoccult												
OTHER	Dental												
	Chest X-ray												
	EKG												
	Glaucoma												
IMMUNIZ	Influenza												
	Tetanus/Diptheria												
	Rubella												
PT. ED.	Breast Self Exam.												

Med. Form #7 Rev. 3/77

Figure D.2

THE DR. MARTIN LUTHER KING, JR.
HEALTH CENTER

ADULT INTAKE / UPDATE HISTORY

DATE: _____

REVIEWER: _____

DEMOGRAPHIC:

Household No. _____ _____
             Adults   Children

Current Occupation: _____

Marital Status; _____

for _____ years.

Highest level of education: _____

PAST HISTORY/FAMILY HISTORY:
Please check (√) if you or a family member
has or had any of these conditions.

	PATIENT	FATHER	MOTHER	BROTHERS SISTERS	CHILDREN	OTHERS
DIABETES						
HIGH BLOOD PRESSURE						
HEART DISEASE						
STROKE						
CANCER						
GLAUCOMA OR BLINDNESS						
T. B.						
ALCOHOLISM OR PROBLEM DRINKER						
NERVOUS BREAKDOWN OR SUICIDE						
HEPATITIS						
URINARY INFECTION OR KIDNEY DISEASE						
PNEUMONIA OR LUNG DISEASE						
RHEUMATIC FEVER OR HEART MURMUR						
SEIZURES OR EPILEPSY						
ASTHMA, HAY FEVER						

Are there any other major medical problems you have seen a doctor about? ☐ Yes ☐ No

Please list them: _____

_____

_____

_____

Date of last tetanus immunization _____
(Approximate Year)

HOSPITALIZATIONS, SURGERY, OR MAJOR INJURIES

WHERE TREATED
(Hospital & Address)

APPROXIMATE DATE

FORM NO. 129 REV. 5/74

Figure D.2 (cont.)

Circle Ⓝ for no, Ⓨ for yes.

1. Are you allergic to penicillin?   1. N   Y

2. Are you allergic to other medicines or substances?   2. N   Y

    If so, which? _____   _____

PLEASE LIST MEDICATIONS YOU COMMONLY USE
(Including Birth Control Pills, Aspirin, Laxatives)

_____

_____

_____

What method of family planning are you currently using? (Please Circle)	Pills IUD (loop) Tied Tubes Diaphragm	Foam Condom (Rubber) Rhythm Vasectomy	Other None

	Beer N Y	_____
Do you drink any alcohol?	Wine N Y	_____
	Liquor N Y	_____

Do you smoke cigarettes?   N   Y   _____ packs per day for _____ years.

SOCIAL HISTORY
Within the last few months or
since we last updated your health
history, have you or has someone close
to you . . . .   COMMENTS

1. Married, Separated, or Divorced?   1. N   Y

2. Become pregnant?   2. N   Y

3. Born or Died?   3. N   Y

4. Or otherwise been added to or left the household?   4. N   Y

5. Become seriously ill?   5. N   Y

6. Changed or lost a job, dropped out of or graduated from
   school, or retired?   6. N   Y

7. Had a significant increase or decrease in income?   7. N   Y

8. Planning to or actually moved?   8. N   Y

*9. Been using heroin, uppers or downers?   9. N   Y

*10. Had trouble with the law?   10. N   Y

11. Have you had trouble with your housing, heat, electricity, or
    plumbing?   11. N   Y

*Recording of this information is left to the discretion of the practitioner.

Figure D.3

THE DR. MARTIN LUTHER KING, JR.
HEALTH CENTER
REVIEW OF SYSTEMS

Date _____ Reviewer _____

Circle Ⓝ for no, Ⓨ for yes. If you do not understand a question, leave blank.

COMMENTS BY REVIEWER
(number your comments according to question number)

CONSTITUTIONAL

1. Do you have any trouble with your appetite?	1. N Y
2. Have you had more than a 10 lb. change in weight in the last year?	2. N Y
3. Do you have fevers or sweats?	3. N Y

SKIN

4. Do you have any skin rashes or sores or itching?	4. N Y
5. Do you have any moles or beauty marks that are changing or are troubling you?	5. N Y

EENT

6. Do you have eye problems or trouble with your vision?	6. N Y
7. Do you have any problems with your ears or with your hearing?	7. N Y
8. Do you have any trouble with your teeth, gums or have any mouth sores?	8. N Y
9. Do you have any sinus trouble?	9. N Y

RESPIRATORY

10. Do you have a persistent cough or phlegm production?	10. N Y
11. Do you ever have any wheezing?	11. N Y
12. Do you ever cough up blood?	12. N Y

CARDIAC

13. Do you have trouble with your breathing?	13. N Y
14. Do you ever have a pain or tightness in your chest?	14. N Y
15. Do your ankles swell?	15. N Y

GASTROINTESTINAL

16. Do you have any difficulty swallowing?	16. N Y
17. Do you have any stomach pains, heartburn, or vomiting?	17. N Y
18. Do you have constipation or use a laxative often?	18. N Y
19. Do you have frequent diarrhea?	19. N Y
20. Have you passed any tarry, black or bloody bowel movements?	20. N Y
21. Has there been any change in color, size or consistency of your bowel movements recently?	21. N Y
22. Do you have rectal hemmorhoids?	22. N Y

GENITOURINARY

23. Do you get up more than once at night to urinate?	23. N Y
24. Do you have any burning sensation with urination?	24. N Y
25. Have you passed any red or dark urine?	25. N Y
26. Do you have trouble starting or stopping your urine?	26. N Y
27. Do you ever lose your urine accidentally when you cough or sneeze?	27. N Y

FORM NO. 128   REV. 5/74

Figure D.3 (cont.)

Circle Ⓝ for no, Ⓨ for yes
If you do not understand a question, leave blank

WOMEN WITH MENSTRUAL PERIODS

28. Date of last monthly period _____
29. Do you have any change in your monthly cycle?   29. N   Y
30. Do you have excessive menstrual bleeding or a period longer than 6 days?   30. N   Y
31. Do you have any vaginal bleeding between your periods or after sexual intercourse?   31. N   Y
32. Are you bothered by a vaginal discharge or vaginal itching, sores or lumps?   32. N   Y
33. Do you have any questions about your sexual functioning?   33. N   Y
34. Do you have any breast lumps, discharge or pain?   34. N   Y

WOMEN WITHOUT MENSTRUAL PERIODS

35. Are you bothered by hot flashes?   35. N   Y
36. Do you ever have any vaginal bleeding or spotting?   36. N   Y
37. Are you bothered by a vaginal discharge or vaginal itching,   37. N   Y
38. Do you have any questions about your sexual functioning?   38. N   Y
39. Do you have any breast lumps, discharge or pain?   39. N   Y
40. Do you examine your breasts monthly?   40. N   Y

MALE — SEXUAL

41. Do you have, any discharge or drip from your penis?   41. N   Y
42. Do you have a sore or a lump on or near your penis?   42. N   Y
43. Do you have any questions about your sexual functioning?   43. N   Y

MUSCULO — SKELETAL

44. Are you bothered by pains in your back, arms, legs or joints?   44. N   Y
45. Do you have any numbness, tingling or weakness in your arms or legs?   45. N   Y

NEUROLOGIC — HEMATOLOGIC

46. Are you bothered by frequent headaches?   46. N   Y
47. Do you have fainting or falling out spells?   47. N   Y
48. Do you bleed or bruise easily?   48. N   Y

EMOTIONAL

49. Do you often feel depressed or sad?   49. N   Y
50. Are you upset or nervous more than you feel you should be?   50. N   Y
51. Do you have trouble sleeping?   51. N   Y
52. Have you had any serious trouble with your memory?   52. N   Y

Figure D.4

THE DR. MARTIN LUTHER KING JR.
HEALTH CENTER

ADULT INTAKE / UPDATE PHYSICAL

DATE: _____

Height _____   Temperature _____

Weight_____   Heart Rate_____

Ideal Weight _____   Visual Acuity R _____ L _____

B.P._____

NEG. NOT DONE

Skin, Hair. . . . . ☐ ☐
Adenopathy . . . . ☐ ☐
Eyes . . . . ☐ ☐
Fundi . . . . ☐ ☐
ENT . . . . ☐ ☐
Teeth, Gums . . . . ☐ ☐
Neck, Thyroid . . . . ☐ ☐
Breasts . . . . ☐ ☐

Breasts self exam taught
  yes   no
  ☐   ☐

Chest. . . . . ☐ ☐
Heart . . . . ☐ ☐
Abdomen. . . . . ☐ ☐
Genitalia, Pelvic . . . . ☐ ☐

Pap   GC Cult.
yes   no   yes   no
☐   ☐   ☐   ☐

Rectal . . . . ☐ ☐
Stool Hematest. . . . . ☐ ☐
Prostate . . . . ☐ ☐
Extremities . . . . ☐ ☐
Peripheral Pulses . . . . ☐ ☐
Neurologic: DTR's . . . . ☐ ☐
Neurologic: Other . . . . ☐ ☐
Mental Status . . . . ☐ ☐

FORM NO. 127 REV. 5/74

_____
Practitioner

Figure D.4 (cont.)

DEFINITION OF TERMS FOR PHYSICAL

Height & Weight: Shoes off

Ideal Weights for Men Ages 25 & Over   **Ideal Weights for Women Ages 25 & Over**

Weight in Pounds According to Frame (In Indoor Clothing)

Height without Shoes Feet	Inches	Small Frame	Medium Frame	Large Frame	Height without Shoes Feet	Inches	Small Frame	Medium Frame	Large Frame
5	1	112–120	118–129	126–141	4	8	92–98	96–107	104–119
5	2	115–123	121–133	129–144	4	9	94–101	98–110	106–122
5	3	118–126	124–136	132–148	4	10	96–104	101–113	109–125
5	4	121–129	127–139	135–152	4	11	99–107	104–116	112–128
5	5	124–133	130–143	138–156	5	0	102–110	107–119	115–131
5	6	128–137	134–147	142–161	5	1	105–113	110–122	118–134
5	7	132–141	138–152	147–166	5	2	108–116	113–126	121–138
5	8	136–145	142–156	151–170	5	3	111–119	116–130	125–142
5	9	140–150	146–160	155–174	5	4	114–123	120–135	129–146
5	10	144–154	150–165	159–179	5	5	118–127	124–139	133–150
5	11	148–158	154–170	164–184	5	6	122–131	128–143	137–154
6	0	152–162	158–175	168–189	5	7	126–135	132–147	141–158
6	1	156–167	162–180	173–194	5	8	130–140	136–151	145–163
6	2	160–171	167–185	178–199	5	9	134–144	140–155	149–168
6	3	164–175	172–190	182–204	5	10	138–148	144–159	153–173

Derived from New Weight Standards for Men and Women, Metropolitan Life Insurance Company Statistical Bulletin, 40:1, 1959
These body weights have been observed to be associated with the lowest mortality rates.

Heart Rate: radial or apical pulse.

Blood Pressure: specify arm and position.

Visual Acuity: use Snellen chart, with glasses if worn.

FOR THE FOLLOWING "NEGATIVE" MEANS:

Skin – no significant lesions or scars.

Hair – no significant abnormalities.

Adenopathy – no significant enlargement of cervical, supraclavicular, axillary or inguinal nodes.

Eyes – no gross abnormalities of conjunctivae, sclerae, irises, lens or corneae. No cataracts. Specify arcus in patients under 50.

Fundi – no significant abnormality of vessels, disks, retinae viewed with funduscope on undilated pupil.

Ears – normal canals and tympanic membranes; no significant cerumen on otoscopic exam. No gross hearing deficit.

Nose – no significant external abnormalities.

Throat – no tonsillar enlargement, no mucosal lesions or abnormal papillation of tongue.

Teeth, Gums – no obvious caries, periodontal disease or dentures.

Neck, Thyroid – no significant masses; no enlargement of thyroid.

Breasts – no abnormalities on inspection and palpation.

Heart – no gallops, significant murmurs or other abnormalities by auscultation.

Abdomen – no hernias, no palpable masses or organomegaly.

Genitalia, Pelvic – Males: no inguinal hernia, no abnormality of penis, testes, or scrotum.

Females: no abnormalities of external or internal genitalia on speculum and manual exam.

Pap and GC Culture – a check in box means that the standard pap with endo and exocervical smears were taken. GC culture from cervix and rectum were done on women under 50.

Rectal – no external abnormality by inspection, digital exam unremarkable.

Stool Hematest – see test package for instructions and definition of negative.

Prostate – no nodules or abnormality of size or consistency.

Extremities – no edema, significant varicose veins, clubbing; no gross abnormalities of bones and joints.

Peripheral pulses – presence and symmetry of dorsalis pedis pulses; if D.P. are absent, posterial tibials can substitute.

Neurologic – DTR's within normal limits in knees and ankles.

Neurologic, Other – This further exam is not required on asymptomatic persons without a history of neurologic disease.

Mental Status – no gross abnormalities of behavior.

Appendix E

Prenatal Care Protocol

Dr. Martin Luther King Jr. Health Center

Prepared by the Nurse Practitioner Women's Health Care Committee and the Ob-Gyn Department.

I. *Initial Data Base*
   A. *History*
      1. Personal history of the patient to include:
         a. Medical with special reference to these conditions: T.B., heart disease, hypertension, diabetes, mental illness, allergies, asthma, german measles, V.D., nephritis, hepatitis, frequent headaches, smoking, and drug abuse.
         b. Surgical.
         c. Obstetrical review of all pregnancies with course and outcome; details to include problems of labor and delivery, postpartum problems, problems of the neonate, and parity.
         d. Menstrual history.
         e. Family planning history.
      2. Family history
         Special references to any condition likely to affect the child or mother; e.g., T.B., diabetes, heart disease, hypertension, mental illness, german measles, allergies, asthma, genetic problems, or multiple births.
      3. History of current pregnancy
         a. last menstrual period, quickening felt.
         b. signs and symptoms patient has experienced since onset of pregnancy.

B. *Physical Examination*
   1. Temperature, pulse, respiration, blood pressure, weight, height.
   2. HEENT, including dental with referral to dentist if necessary.
   3. Neck—palpation of cervical nodes and thyroid.
   4. Percussion and auscultation of heart and lungs.
   5. Circulation—cervical, radial, femoral and pedal pulses.
   6. Back—spinal deformities, CVA tenderness.
   7. Breast examination, including axillary nodes. Teach breast self examination.
   8. Abdomen—liver, spleen, masses, scars, hernias.
   9. Palpation and percussion to determine height of fundus.
   10. Extremities—check for edema, varicosities, deformities, range of motion.
   11. Vaginal examination with Pap smear and culture for gonorrhea. Pelvic evaluation.
C. *Laboratory Workup*
   1. Urinalysis (mid-stream clean catch)—first visit and at 32 weeks. Also, at each clinic visit check urine for sugar, acetone, and protein.
   2. Serology—first visit, with repeat at 32 weeks. See VD protocol for treatment as necessary.
   3. Blood type, Rh type, and antibody screening.
   4. CBC, sickle cell prep. Repeat hematocrit at 32 weeks gestation. If positive sickle prep, order hemoglobin electrophoresis and offer testing of partner and other information as appropriate.
   5. PPD routinely. Do not give if patient had BCG vaccine or previously positive tuberculin test. Instead, refer to internist.
   6. Chest x-ray is not done routinely. If no previous chest x-ray in chart or if medically indicated (e.g., positive tuberculin test, pneumonia, cardiac condition, sarcoidosis), consult physician. If chest x-ray is done an abdominal shield should be used.

II. *Medications and Management of Common Problems*

Instruct the patient to take no medications except those prescribed by a physician or nurse practitioner, and to always state that she is pregnant when receiving medical care.

A. Routine Medications

    1. Prenatal vitamins (contain calcium and 1 mg folic acid) one tablet q.d. (If patient cannot tolerate large vitamin tablets give multi-vitamins together with 1 mg folic acid O.D. and encourage to drink milk. May also try liquid vitamins.)

    2. Ferrous sulfate 300 mg or Ferrous Gluconate 300 mg t.i.d. If patient cannot tolerate Fe tablets try liquid iron or spansules.

B. Morning sickness

    1. AM routine—advise dry biscuits, toast, or crackers in early morning and/or suck hard candy or ice cubes. Avoid fluids and greasy foods. If this fails try #2.

    2. Bendectin 2 tabs. HS and 1 tab. AM. If not successful or if hyperemesis suspected, refer to or consult with obstetrician.

C. Heartburn

Antacid. Warn patient against using Bromoseltzer and Alkaseltzer (contain salicylates).

D. Constipation

    1. Diet counselling

    2. If further treatment is needed use any of the following:

        a. Colace 100 mg HS to be taken with lots of water daily.

        b. Milk of magnesia 30 cc HS prn if colace is ineffective.

        c. Metamucil 1 tsp. in 1 full glass of water, milk or juice.

        d. Glycerine suppositories.

        e. Mineral oil retention enema.

E. Headaches without other symptoms

    1. Evaluate blood pressure, fundi, investigate stress sources.

2. Advise rest and relaxation, cold cloth to head, back rub, etc. Tylenol 300 mg., 2 tabs t.i.d. prn. *Unrelenting headache should be reevaluated within 3 days.*

F. Insomnia
    1. Massages, warm baths at bedtime, walk.
    2. Consult obstetrician if medication is needed.
G. Anxiety
    1. Listening, counselling. Involve Family Health Worker regarding social problems as necessary.
    2. Phenobarbital may be used after counselling patient and consultation with team internist or obstetrician.
H. Leg cramps
    Check milk intake and increase if inadequate.
I. Pain in lower abdomen—after eliminating the possibility of organic problem advise patient to wear maternity girdle. May also apply heat source and, when resting, lie on same side as pain.
J. Low back pain—eliminate the possibility of organic problem. Advise maternity girdle, bed board, exercise.
K. Pain and tenderness in breasts—advise well fitting supporting bra.
L. Diet—emphasize high protein, fresh fruits and vegetables, sufficient fluids.
M. Hygiene
    1. Any type shower or bath permitted (do not take bath after rupture or leaking of membranes or bloody show).
    2. Douching only as prescribed, then douche reclining in bathtub with douche bag lowered to reduce water stream pressure.
    3. 1-2 hours mid-day rest period with feet elevated.
    4. Sexual activity as comfortable until onset of labor.

III. *Continuing Data Base and Management*
    A. The patient is seen every four weeks during the first 28 weeks, every two weeks up to the 36th week and every week thereafter until delivery, unless otherwise indicated.

B. Reexamination includes: urinalysis, weight, blood pressure, examination of extremities, height of fundus, fetal heart and position. It also includes teaching, exploring interest in prenatal classes, determining family planning method to be used after delivery, if desired. Instruction and discussion regarding preparation of the mother and family for the new baby should be carried on throughout pregnancy.

C. Patient should be referred to an obstetrician for an examination prior to the 20th week of pregnancy and again within the 34th-36th weeks.

D. Instruct patient regarding breast care. If she intends to nurse baby, give more detailed information.

E. Complete obstetrical information card as soon as lab data is complete and give copy to patient (see p. 230). Determine hospital where patient wishes to deliver and send her for registration if appropriate; advise of transportation arrangements and how to contact obstetrician.

F. Complete prenatal record, including lab data, so that it can be photostated at 34 to 36 weeks by maternity records coordinator and sent to hospital of choice.

G. Enter name, chart number, address, expected date of confinement, and hospital on prenatal list and forward list to maternity records coordinator monthly.

IV. *Special Problems*

A. Vaginitis—See vaginitis protocol. Treat if symptomatic or in presence of eroded cervix.

1. Monilia—Mycostatin vaginal suppositories (100,000 units); 1 suppository b.i.d. for 10-14 days. If suspicious of diabetes, 2 hour post-prandial blood sugar essential. Mycostatin Cream may be used externally as indicated.

2. Trichomonas—Flagyl is contraindicated in pregnancy. Sultrin suppositories b.i.d. for 10 days. If symptoms persist try low pressure betadine douche reclining in bathtub.

3. Non-specific—Sultrin Cream or suppositories HS or b.i.d. for 10 days; when using Sultrin after 36 weeks consult with obstetrician first.

B. Anemia—Review diet history and intake of iron.
Anyone with hematocrit of 32 percent or below should have CBC and reticulocyte count, be reinstructed in proper iron and folate intake, and be checked for response in 2 weeks. If response is unsatisfactory or if hematocrit of 30 percent or below, order sickle cell prep if not previously done, G6PD, stool for guaiac, ova and parasites, serum iron, total iron binding capacity and consult with the physician about follow-up.

C. Diabetes
For the diabetic pregnant woman frequent follow up and careful control are essential and the patient should be followed from the beginning by the nurse practitioner-internist-obstetrician team. To detect gestational diabetes do fasting and 2 hour post-prandial blood sugar and repeat in each trimester for patients with:
1. History of diabetes in family.
2. History of 8½ pound or heavier baby.
3. History of stillbirths or other reproductive disasters.
4. Asymptomatic bacteriuria.
5. Obesity.
6. Spilling sugar.
7. Polyhydramnios.
8. Persistent monilial vaginitis.

D. Rh negative
1. Verify accuracy of report.
2. Test father's Rh and type.
3. a. If patient has negative titer, repeat again at 32 weeks.
    b. If patient has positive titer, or history of previous Rh difficulty, inform obstetrician, repeat titer every month during the first 30 weeks, then every two weeks until delivery if there is no evidence of a rise in titer.
    c. If patient has a rising titer, refer immediately to the obstetrician.

E. If Rh positive antibody titer, repeat both tests to

verify accuracy, and ask for identification of antibody. Discuss with obstetrician.

Obstetrician should be consulted regarding the following:

1. Blood pressure greater than 140/90
2. A gradual rise in blood pressure
3. Albumin in urine (above trace or persistent trace repeat morning specimen first)
4. Marked weight gain
5. Pylonephritis or simple urinary tract infections
6. Rh negative problems
7. Abnormal lie at term; head not descended
8. Signs of toxemia; persistent dizziness, headaches, edema, etc.
9. Severe varicosities
10. Phlebitis
11. Hyperemesis gravidarum
12. Resistant vaginitis/cervical erosion
13. Abnormal Pap smear findings
14. Positive serology
15. Any medical condition listed under history taking
16. More than 2 weeks past expected date of delivery
17. Question of ruptured membranes—do slide test and/ or pH first. To do slide test take a specimen of leaking fluid by pressing glass against perineum or examining table where fluid has spilled. Dry without moving slide (takes 15 minutes). Examine slide for crystalization in a fern pattern which identifies amniotic fluid. Also, can check pH of fluids with nitrazine paper; amniotic fluid will be alkaline.
18. Condyloma acuminata
19. Bleeding at any stage of pregnancy, with or without pain
20. Abdominal pain—persistent, severe
21. Absence of fetal heart sounds after six months gestation
22. Previous caesarian sections
23. Multiple spontaneous abortions or history of infertility
24. Question of multiple gestation

Internist should also evaluate with the nurse practitioner and obstetrician:

1. Anemia
2. Phlebitis and varicosities
3. Asthma and allergies
4. Seizures
5. Diabetes
6. Kidney problems
7. Cardiac problems
8. Cholecystitis
9. Ulcers
10. Other serious conditions

V. *Counselling and teaching during pregnancy*
  A. First trimester
    1. Signs and symptoms of early pregnancy—what to expect; e.g., frequency of urination, nausea, vomiting, etc.
    2. Physiological changes to expect; e.g., breast size, changes in pigmentation, etc.
    3. Morning sickness (see recommendations under section II).
    4. Diet—emphasize a balanced diet.
    5. Give pertinent literature to patient.
    6. Hygiene—no vaginal douches unless ordered by doctor.
    7. No restrictions on activities of daily living, unless medically indicated.
    8. Explore feelings about pregnancy and acceptance of new baby into the family.
  B. Second trimester
    1. Review anatomy of female reproductive system.
    2. Explanation of developing fetus.
    3. Discuss Braxton Hicks contractions.
    4. Preparation of family and home for the new baby; e.g., discuss sibling rivalry.
    5. Special breast care in preparation for breast feeding.

C. Third trimester
   1. Review family planning—focus on method of interest to patient.
   2. Review preparation for baby: sleeping arrangements, layette, "babysitter" for other children during puerperium.
   3. Symptoms of pregnancy for last trimester; e.g., discomforts, frequency of urination, lightening, etc.
   4. Discuss sexual activity of patient after 36th week if indicated.
   5. Preparation for labor and delivery.
   6. Hospital routine—enema, vaginal exams, etc.
   7. Breathing technique and exercises.
   8. Explanation of post-partum home visit within 48 hours of discharge from hospital. Advise patient to contact team on or before discharge.
   9. Paternity papers should be signed if indicated.

VI. *Recording* (see form, pp. 226-229)
   1. Date and sign history on front sheet of prenatal re-record.
   2. Indicate nurse and family health worker in upper part of prenatal record.
   3. Hospital choice on front page of prenatal record.
   4. All entries on prenatal record to be signed.
   5. Add name to your prenatal list after patient's first visit; indicate date of last menstrual period and expected date of confinement. Updated list is sent to maternity records coordinator monthly.
   6. Use of Weed System when applicable.
   7. Flag all emergency or warning information in red on front of chart and on photostated copy (e.g., allergies to drugs, C-sections, Rh negative).

Figure E.1

THE DR. MARTIN LUTHER KING JR. HEALTH CENTER — **PRENATAL RECORD** — TEL.: 992-9100

TEAM: _____ MLK #: _____   PHYSICIAN: _____ EXT. ____

NAME: _____   NURSE PRACTITIONER: _____ EXT. ____

ADDRESS: _____   FAMILY HEALTH WORKER: _____ EXT. ____

RELIGION: _____ AGE: _____   EMERGENCY CONTACT: _____

PHONE: _____ B. D.: _____   ADDRESS: _____

PREVIOUS OBSTETRICAL HISTORY   isoimmunization   Eclampsia No ☐   Hemorrhage No ☐   Hypert. No ☐   Rh or ABO No ☐

No. of Preg.	YEAR	PLACE OF CONFINEMENT	Duration of Gestation	Duration of Labor	Type of Delivery	Cond. of Child at Birth	Birth Wgt. of Child	
1								
2								Hospital For Delivery
3								
4								
5								
6								
7								REGISTERED_____
8								
9								Family Planning Method Wanted
10								
11								Yes ☐ No ☐
12								Type

SUMMARY NO. OF:	FULL TERM	PREMATURE	MULT. BIRTHS	ABORTION	NOW ALIVE	MENARCHE MENSES IRR ☐ REG ☐

PRESENT PREGNANCY   Give dates of: Est. Date of   Planned Pregnancy
Last Menstruation   Quickening   Confinement   Yes ☐ No ☐
Accepted _____ Happy _____

Family Planning History: Special Problems

FAMILY HISTORY

TBC	HYPERTENSION	HEART DISEASE	DIABETES	EPILEPSY NEURO/PSYCH	ALLERGIES	GENETIC PROBLEMS	MULTI BIRTHS

MEDICAL HISTORY OF PATIENT	CHECK IF POSITIVE	REMARKS
NEPHRITIS OR FREQ. UTI		
HEART DISEASE OR HX OF M		
HYPERTENSION		
TUBERCULOSIS, BCG OR PPD.		
SYPHILIS GC. OTHER VD		
CIG		
GYN. DISEASE		
GERMAN MEASLES		
OTHER VIRUS DISEASES		
DIABETES		
THYROID DISFUNCTION		
PHLEBITIS OR VARICOSITIES		
PNEUMONIA		
RHEUMATIC TRIAD		
FREQUENT HEADACHES		
EMOTIONAL PROBLEMS		
EPILEPSY		
DRUG SENSITIVITY		
OTHER ALLERGIES		
BLOOD DYSCRASIA		
BLOOD TRANSFUSIONS		HISTORY BY: _____ DATE: _____
OPERATIONS & ACCIDENTS		
DRUGS/ALCOHOL		CHART XEROXED BY: _____ DATE: _____

FORM NO. MED. 9 MLK. REV. 11/74

Figure E.1 (cont.)

NAME _____

PHYSICAL EXAMINATION
General
Nutrition

T.	P.	R.	B.P.	Hgt.	Pres. Wgt.	Usual Wght.	

Eyes _____ Teeth _____ Throat _____ Thyroid _____

Heart _____ Nose _____ Ears _____ Gross Hearing _____

Lungs _____ Nodes _____

Breasts _____ Nipples _____ Tumors _____

Abdomen _____

Fetal Heart _____ Est. Fetal Wgt. _____ Presentation and Pos. _____ Duration of Preg. _____

Orthopedic Defects _____ Varicosities _____

Extremities _____ Deep Tendon Reflexes _____ Edema _____

Periphal Pulses C___ ___ R___ ___ F___ ___ DP___ ___

Vision (R) (L)
W/O 20/ 20/
Glasses

PELVIC EXAMINATION

Vulva _____ Bartholin Glands _____ Urethra (Skenes Glands) _____

Vagina _____

    Anterior Wall (Normal Relaxed) _____ Cystocele (Small, Moderate, Large) _____

    Posterior Wall (Normal Relaxed) _____ Rectocele (Small, Moderate, Large) _____

Perineum (Intact, Repaired, Lacerated) _____ Support (Good, Poor) _____

Cervix _____

Uterus _____

Adnexae, Right _____ Left _____

RECTAL EXAMINATION

    Presence of Stricture   Yes ☐   No ☐

PELVIC MEASUREMENTS

Diag. Conj. ___ cm; Transv. Diam. of Outlet ___ cm; Shape of Sacrum ___ ; Arch (Wide, Acute) _____

Prominence of Spines   Yes ☐   No ☐

Examined By: _____ , N. P. _____ Date _____ , M. D. _____ Date

LABORATORY FINDINGS

SICKLE CELL ☐ POS (HGB) ☐ NEG

DATE	HCRT	VDRL	ABO TYPE	RH	ANTIB TITER	RUBEL TITER	HR. PPBS	U/A S	A	P			TINE	GC	PAP		

TEACHINGS	FIRST TRI			SECOND TRI			THIRD TRI	
DIET - HYGIENE			ANATOMY & PHYSIOLOGY			PHYSIOLOGIC CHANGES		
ACTIVITY - SEX			FETAL DEVELOPMENT			COMMON DISCOMFORTS		
PERSON/FAM. ACCEPTANCE			BRAXTON HICKS CONTR.			LABOR & DELIVERY		
PHYSIOLOGIC CHANGES			FAMILY PLANNING			EXERCISE/BREATHING		
COMMON DISCOMFORTS			BREAST CARE			HOSPITAL PROCEDURE		
LITERATURE			PREP. OF FAM. & HOME			READINESS EMOT./THINGS		
PRENATAL CARE ROUTINE			SIBLING RIVALRY			POST PARTUM		

228

Figure E.1 (cont.)

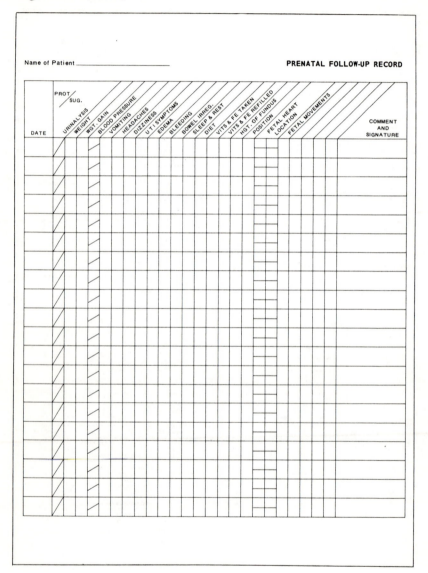

Name of Patient _____   **PRENATAL FOLLOW-UP RECORD**

DATE	PROT/SUG. URINALYSIS	WEIGHT	WGT. GAIN	BLOOD PRESSURE	VOMITING	HEADACHES	DIZZINESS	U.T.I SYMPTOMS	EDEMA	BLEEDING	BOWEL IRREG.	SLEEP & REST	DIET	VITS & FE TAKEN	VITS & FE REFILLED	HGT. OF FUNDUS	POSITION	FETAL HEART	LOCATION	FETAL MOVEMENTS	COMMENT AND SIGNATURE

Figure E.1 (cont.)

PRENATAL RECORD – Continued

Name of Patient

MEDICATIONS: NAME AND DOSES	DATES					
	START	END	START	END	START	END

DATE	PROGRESS NOTES AND CONSULTATIONS

Figure E.2   Patient Obstetrical Information Card

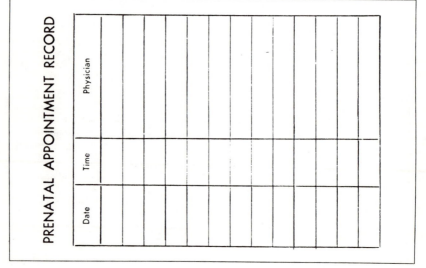

THE DR. MARTIN LUTHER KING, JR. HEALTH CENTER

EMERGENCY OBSTETRICAL INFORMATION

I.D. # _____

NAME_____AGE_____RELIGION_____

ADDRESS_____APT._____PHONE NO. _____

NEAREST RELATIVE _____RELATIONSHIP_____

ADDRESS_____APT_____PHONE NO._____

L.M.P._____E.D.C._____PREV. PREG.: FT._____PREM. _____AB._____LIVE_____

BLOOD: TYPE_____Rh_____Titer_____   Hmt._____Serology_____

COMPLICATIONS PRESENT PREGNANCY:

  Toxemia _____Diabetes_____Heart Disease _____
  Drug Allergy_____Multiple Gestation _____
  Others (Specify) _____

COMPLICATIONS POST PREGNANCY:

ALWAYS CARRY THIS CARD WITH YOU
SIEMPRE LLEVE CONSIGO ESTA TARJETA

FORM NO. MED. 13 M.L.K. REV. 1976

PRENATAL APPOINTMENT RECORD

Physician

Time

Date

Appendix F

Instructions for Making HySS Card on Hypertensives Registered and Known To Be Hypertensive Prior to 10/1/75

Patient is hypertensive if:
>Age 20-49: BP greater than 140/90
>Age 50 and over: BP greater than 160/95

Patient must:
>a. be over 20 yrs. of age (born before 1956)
>b. not be pregnant
>c. have had 1 visit to MLK since 9/15/73
>d. not have died prior to 10/1/75

I. *Classification of registered hypertensives prior to 10/1/75*

>A. ↑ BP on problem list, on one or more antihypertensive meds (including HCTZ)

>B. ↑ BP on problem list, on no diuretics or antihypertensive
>>1. Average last 3 diastolics—if greater than values listed above, add to study; or
>>2. Average last 3 systolics—if greater than values listed above, add to study.

>C. ↑ BP *not* on problem list, if in last 3 visits, patient is on antihypertensives other than diuretics, add to study.

>D. ↑ BP not on problem list, if only on diuretics, add to study *if*
>>1. One of the last 3 visits has hypertensive note, and there is no indication that diuretics are being used for other problems e.g., cyclic edema, ascites, etc.

or

2. Average of last 3 BP's systolic or diastolic is greater than limits.

E. ↑ BP *not* on problem list, not on diuretics or antihypertensives.

   1. Average of last 3 BP's systolic or diastolic is greater than limits.

II. *Items to be printed on the HySS card starting in the upper left hand corner (see p. 237)*

   *1. Name

   *2. Chart no.

   3. Race (if last name is hispanic, check hispanic; if last name is not hispanic, check non-hispanic)

   4. Sex—M or F

   5. Birth date

   6. Age as of 10/1/75 (do *not* put age as of date of filling in the card)

   *7. Team (put the name of the team of the family health worker to whom the patient is assigned; if the patient is on Team M, put letter M plus name of team of the *physician* whom patient is seeing)

   *8. Address

   *9. Out-of-Area (see map on unit or contact HySS operator to determine if address is out-of-area; out-of-area means out of entire MLK boundaries, not just out of a team area)

   *10. Home telephone

   *11. Other telephone

   12. On Medicaid (at time of filling out the card; each unit has a computerized list with Medicaid status)

   *13. Internist name and code (see code sheet)

   *14. FHW name and code (see code sheet)

   *15. NP name and code (see code sheet)

   16. Cardiomegaly on latest x-ray (if necessary check with internist to answer this)

   17. LVH on latest EKG (if necessary check with internist to fill this in)

   18. Date of last BP prior to 10/1/75. Code as follows:

---

*If any of these items change, the team member who notices the change must print in the new information and then report it to the HySS operator for recoding. Change in these items only must be reported.

Code *1*: 0-4.0 mo. prior to 10/1/75. (6/1/75-9/30/75)

Code *2*: 4.1-8.0 mo. prior to 10/1/75 (2/1/75-5/31/75)

Code *3*: 8.1-12.0 mo. prior to 10/1/75 (10/1/74-1/31/75)

Code *4*: 12.1 + mo. prior to 10/1/75 (Before 10/1/75)

19. Prestudy classification (see Section I above and code as A, B, C, D, or E)

20. Last BP prior to 10/1/75—i.e., BP on date recorded in Item 18.
    Check C if this BP controlled (definition above)
    Check U if this BP uncontrolled

21. Weight as of last BP—record weight as of date in Item 18. If no weight recorded, go back in chart until you find one. If none ever recorded, write in: "No weight in chart."
    Overweight: check *yes* if: male > 200 lbs
    female >170 lbs
    check *no* if weighs less than above

22. Antihypertensive diuretic meds prescribed?
    Check *yes* if prescribed, regardless of whether patient is taking them or not

23. If no meds prescribed, no. of BP readings available for determining average. Do not fill this or average BP in if patient has had antihypertensive meds prescribed. Only fill it in if no meds were ever prescribed, i.e., prestudy classification B, D-2 or E. Record number of BP's averaged to get average BP.

24. Average blood pressure

25. Records of visits and blood pressures at the bottom of the HySS card—please record here beginning with first visit after 10/1/75, the day and blood pressure of all subsequent unit visits. This should contain the lowest sitting at rest blood pressure obtained on any particular visit. Do not record BP's taken from ER, FHW, or Specialty Units.

III. Weeding out inactive patients
    Once these previously registered people are identified

from their chart as hypertensive, follow-up of those not seen for 4 months will be attempted for eight weeks. If there is no response in terms of a patient visit, the person's card will be removed from the active file.

Figure F.1

HYPERTENSION SURVEILLANCE SYSTEM CARD

DR. MARTIN LUTHER KING, JR. HEALTH CENTER

PATIENT LAST NAME: Jones   FIRST: Fictisha
PATIENT ADDRESS: 1408 Webster Ave.   APT NO: 25N   CITY: Bronx   STATE: N.Y.   ZIP: 10456
HOME TELEPHONE: 677-7766
BUSINESS TELEPHONE:

CHART NUMBER: 01-123345
BIRTH DATE: 8/6/35   SEX: F   AGE AS OF 10/1/75: 39

INTERNISTS
NURSE PRACTITIONER
FAMILY HEALTH WORKER

H.W. NAME: Cruz   CODE: 3
N.P. NAME: White   CODE: 2
INTERNIST NAME: Smith   CODE: 59

PRE-STUDY CLASSIFICATION
DATE LAST B.P. PRIOR TO 10/1/75
BLOOD PRESSURE BASE LINE
WEIGHT F > 170
RESEARCH CONTROL

ON MEDICAID? Y N
OVERWEIGHT? Y N
WEIGHT AS OF LAST B.P: 180

DATE LAST B.P. PRIOR TO PRE-STUDY CLASSIFICATION 10/1/75: 7/30/75   CODE E
PRE-STUDY CLASSIFICATION: 2
AVERAGE B.P: 165/98

CARDIOMEGALY ON LATEST X-RAY: YES NO
LVH - LATEST EKG: YES NO

DATE PATIENT LEFT STUDY
PATIENT LEFT STUDY
FIRST B.P.

ANTIHYPERTENSIVE / DIURETIC MEDS PRESCRIBED? YES NO
IF NO MEDS PRESCRIBED NO. OF B.P READINGS AVAILABLE? 1 2

PATIENT ADMITTED TO STUDY
DATE WHEN PATIENT ENTERED STUDY

INTRODUCED TO PAT-ED PROGRAM: YES NO
NO. OF ED VISITS: 1 2 3 4 5 6
HYSS F/U
NP ED
F/U +

DATE WHEN NEW PATIENT ENTERED STUDY
REASON FOR LEAVING

VISITS

MONTH	DAY	B.P.	DAY	B.P.	DAY	B.P.
OCT						
NOV	13	160/95				
DEC	12	155/95	27	140/90		
JAN 76						
FEB						
MAR	12	135/85				
APRIL						
MAY	16	130/85				
JUNE	15	140/85				

Figure F.1 (cont.)

Family Health Worker Follow-up
for Hypertensives with No Visit in Four Months

Family Health Workers will receive a photostated HySS card of all patients not seen in 4 months. Date of letters sent, calls made, and home visits must be notated on the photostat of the HySS card. Biweekly the HySS operator will talk with each family health worker and record what they have done on each patient. After the following steps have been made, the patient's HySS card may be removed from the active file.

In Area With Phone

wk 1 Telephone x 2 to speak with person or partner, if no success, night or weekend call encouraged, not required.*

wk 2 If no success, letter No. 1.

wk 3 If no success, home visit with message under door.

wk 4 If no success, letter No. 2 with reply postcard.

wk 5 If no success, remove HySS card from file.

In Area Without Phone
(i.e., no person at Bell Info Central—x411—by that name)

Letter No. 1. wk 1

If no success, letter No. 2 with reply postcard. wk 2

If no success, home visit leaving message under door. wk 3

If no success, letter No. 3. wk 4

If no success, remove HySS card from file. wk 5

Out of Area With Phone

wk 1 Telephone x 2 to speak with person or partner. If no success night or weekend call encouraged, not required.*

wk 2 If no success, letter No. 1.

wk 3 If no success, letter No. 2 with reply postcard.

wk 4 If no success, remove HySS card from file.

Out of Area Without Phone

If no success, letter No. 1. wk 1

If no success, letter No. 2 with reply postcard. wk 2

If no success, letter No. 3. wk 3

If no success, remove HySS card from file. wk 4

*Physicians and nurse practitioners may help out during their evening sessions. Physicians should sign the letters.

Figure F.2

DR. MARTIN LUTHER KING JR. HEALTH CENTER
3674 Third Avenue — Bronx, New York 10456
Telephone: 212-960-2000

Dear

    I have just looked at your medical record here at the Martin Luther King Health Center. It indicates that you have high blood pressure which could be dangerous to your health.

    I would like to work with you to help you get your pressure controlled, but I need to hear from you to see when you're able to come for an appointment.

    Please call   , your Family Health Worker, at 960-2000 extension   to arrange an appointment or to talk with us about problems you're having in coming in. We look forward to hearing from you.

            Sincerely,

1/bm

Figure F.3

DR. MARTIN LUTHER KING JR. HEALTH CENTER
3674 Third Avenue — Bronx, New York 10456
Telephone: 212-960-2000

Dear

    I wrote to you 1-2 weeks ago because our records show that you need an appointment to be seen for your high blood pressure. If you do not get treatment for this problem it can be dangerous to your health.

    As you know, high blood pressure can cause serious damage to your heart, brain and kidneys. It can lead to strokes and is a major factor in sudden death from heart attacks. Unfortunately, high blood pressure is usually a "silent" problem; you may not feel ill in any way until <u>after</u> the serious damage is done.

    Most people need medicines to lower their pressure. The medicines must be taken even when you feel well because your blood pressure can go up without your knowing it. If you have had problems with the medicines your doctor prescribed, it is important for us to know what these problems are so that a better treatment plan can be worked out to avoid serious side effects.

    Proper treatment can keep your blood pressure at a lower, safer level. The only way to know what your blood pressure is, is to have it measured. So, it is urgent that you come in to have it checked.

    Please call   , your Family Health Worker, at 960-2000 extension   so we can make an appointment for you as soon as possible. If you're having trouble calling us, please fill out the attached postcard and drop it in the mail so we know you heard from us.

        Sincerely yours,

2/bm

Att.

242

Figure F.4

Please check or write below:

Date: _____

☐ Please schedule an appointment for me:
I prefer ☐ 9-12 A.M. ☐ 1-5 P.M. ☐ 6-9 P.M.

☐ I am going to another physician or clinic and prefer to continue there.

☐ My phone number is: _____ ☐ I have no phone.

☐ The address you sent is wrong.
I have a new address: _____

_____

Further Comments: _____

_____

_____

Signed: _____

Figure F.5

OFFICE OF ECONOMIC OPPORTUNITY   MONTEFIORE HOSPITAL

DR. MARTIN LUTHER KING JR. HEALTH CENTER

3674 Third Avenue — Bronx, New York 10456
Telephone: 212-960-2000

Dear

    I sent you two letters before concerning the fact that you had high blood pressure and that it was my desire to help you control it. I haven't heard from you and thought that my previous letters may have gotten lost. Since the Team doesn't have a phone listed for you, we decided we'd write again in hopes of reaching you.

    As you probably know, you have high blood pressure. You may feel fine now but over the long run, high blood pressure can cause damage to your heart, kidneys and brain. It's not worth worrying about when medication can make it normal.

    Please come in and I can plan with you some way to make your pressure normal. If you are having any special difficulties coming to the center for treatment or are being treated elsewhere, please let us know.

    You can drop by and make an appointment or call   , your Family Health Worker, at 960-2000 extension   for an appointment. But whatever you do, don't hesitate. Contact us today.

               Sincerely yours,

3/bm